Freed to Serve

By the same author:

Freed to serve

by

Michael Green

HODDER AND STOUGHTON
LONDON · SYDNEY · AUCKLAND · TORONTO

British Library Cataloguing in Publication Data

Green, Michael, *1930–*
   Freed to Serve.
   1. Clergy—Office
   I. Title
   262'.14   BV660.2

ISBN 0 340 28195 2

*Hodder and Stoughton Editorial Office: 47 Bedford Square, London
WC1B 3DP*

CONTENTS

For Timothy and Sarah
and their generation of servant leaders

PREFACE

For many years I have been involved in training men for ministry within the Anglican Church, first as a tutor at the London College of Divinity, then as principal of St. John's College, Nottingham. It has been exceedingly rewarding. It has also driven me back time and again to reflection about first principles in Christian leadership. And in the last six years I have sought to work out those principles in the life of a busy parish.

This book is an examination of those first principles. They seem very radical, because the Christian church has departed so far from the patterns of ministry to be found in the New Testament. We have got a long way away from Jesus the Servant. It is time to take stock and to reform.

Some of this book is a working over of *Called to Serve*, published in 1964: in particular, chapters 5–7. But as the issues discussed there continue to be matters for debate and more frequently still for unexamined assumption in Anglican circles, I hardly think that requires an apology. I have also drawn on unpublished material and a contribution I made to *Obeying Christ in a Changing World* (1977) and am grateful to Hodder & Stoughton and Collins for permission to reissue that material in a completely new form.

The plan of this book is simple. The first four chapters look at New Testament guidelines for ministry in the Christian church. Chapters five to eight look at issues which have long been in dispute concerning the ordained ministry. And the last two chapters show how New Testament principles can be implemented in a modern church within the Anglican Communion. If the result of the book is to drive clergy and congregations to a re-examination of their role in the light of the New Testament, I shall be well satisfied.

I want to express my deep gratitude to my teachers in the New Testament, especially Professor C.F.D. Moule and Dr. Henry Chadwick; to my colleagues in shared ministry first at St. John's College, Nottingham and latterly at St. Aldate's; and to Canon John Tiller, the General Secretary of A.C.C.M., who gave helpful advice on the last two chapters.

Michael Green

CHAPTER ONE

A STUDY IN CONTRASTS

There are few aspects of Christianity which need a more radical reappraisal than the purpose and function of its ministry, if we are going to be obedient to the call and commission of Christ in a fast-changing society. The trouble is twofold: we are disobedient to the directions Christ has given us about ministry, and we are failing to meet the needs of contemporary society. We are missing out at both levels.

Consider the image of the Christian minister in the modern mind. It is perhaps a bit better in America where there is a high level of churchgoing and a great deal of vital Christianity, but in many parts of the Western world the image is deplorable. The Christian minister is thought irrelevant to ordinary life. He is simply there to be called on in the crises of life. He is involved in protest marches. He keeps an ancient building going. He recites services on Sundays but nobody knows what he does for the rest of the week. He is seen as a figure of fun, a meek and mild little fellow attempting to teach Christianity to middle-class women and children but steering clear of the real world of men. He seems to be, and often is, a man unsure of his role in a society that has left him behind.

If Christian leaders are on the whole not very successful at relating to modern society, they are even less successful at implementing the teaching of the New Testament on Christian ministry. There is no single area where we have departed more signally from the indications given in these foundation documents of the early church. Here are a dozen or so of the more obvious contrasts.

1. *In the New Testament, ministry had to be received before it was exercised*. You had to let Christ serve you before you attempted to do anything for Christ. Simon Peter learnt this lesson at the foot washing. He was most indignant at the suggestion that Jesus should wash his feet: thoroughly embarrassing. But he had to learn that unless he allowed Jesus to wash his feet he could have no lot or part with him. This passage (John 13:8ff) enshrines the first basic principle of ministry in the New Testament. Nobody can serve Christ until he first lets Christ serve him. We all have to undergo the humbling, embarrassing business of being washed and cleansed by Jesus. Until then we are useless. But in most churches of the Western world it is perfectly possible to get yourself ordained without having had any vital experience of the cleansing of Christ. You can become a minister of the grace of God without ever having experienced it. No wonder such ministry is ineffective.

2. *In the New Testament, all Christians were called to ministry, not some*. That is astonishing to us! We have grown used to the idea that there are the ordinary Christians, who sit in the pew on Sundays, and the extra-special Christians who become missionaries or clergy or nuns. Somehow they are different. They, and not the rest of us, are the ones called to serve. When we think of Christian ministry today we instinctively think of a man ordained to the ministry of the word and the sacraments. So you either are a minister or you are not.

It was very different in New Testament days. They knew nothing of any such distinction. All Christians are called to serve Christ, all are commissioned for ministry. We shall be looking at this further in a subsequent chapter. It is, to our shame, sufficiently revolutionary a concept to need further expansion. But for the moment it is sufficient to emphasise that for the New Testament writers the Christian ministry is coextensive with the Christian church.

3. *In the New Testament, ministry was a function, not a status*. It was a verb, not a noun. We have got ourselves tied up in talk about indelible character in ordination and the

like: they spoke of the need by love to serve one another, to bear one another's burdens and so fulfil the law of Christ. Jesus had drawn the contrast between the world's ideas of leadership and his own. 'The kings of the Gentiles exercise lordship over them . . . But not so with you; rather let the greatest among you become as the youngest, and the leader as one who serves . . . I am among you as one who serves.' (Luke 22:25–27) It is not the status of the agent but the nature of the action which constitutes Christian ministry.

4. *In the New Testament, ministry was something corporate and shared*. With us it is nearly always exercised singly or at best in pairs. We never find a presbyter in the singular in the New Testament. Always he is a member of a team. This was true of the apostles themselves; the twelve functioned as a team, and they set up local leadership in the same way. We refuse to follow their example, and then complain because our minister fails to be omnicompetent. This is a serious situation. It is bad for the man himself to be made to feel he is the sole minister. It may lead to despair, arrogance, blindness to the realities of a situation, or inhibiting the gifts of others. It is bad for the church members. They may well become critical and lazy. When the different limbs in Christ's body are not allowed to exercise their God-given ministry, they are harmed and their gifts atrophy. Team leadership is much harder to achieve, but much more fulfilling for one and all when it is achieved. It is, moreover, as we shall see later on, practical politics in any church, however small.

5. *In the New Testament authorisation followed ministry rather than preceded it*. We tend to think of ministry as something exercised in and for the church only after proper authorisation. The early Christians saw all ministry as a gift from the ascended Christ for his Body through one of its members; the authorisation followed once a person had shown that he had received the gift. If we think about it at all, we assume that the ordination will convey the gift. All too often it does not!

6. *In New Testament days, character, not intellect, was the most important condition*. If you look at the qualities laid down for those who would exercise oversight in Christian assemblies (Titus 1:5–9; 1 Tim. 3:1–13; 1 Pet. 5:1–5) you will find that they do not concentrate on passing examinations and collecting an adequate amount of book learning. Instead they are much more concerned with the person's maturity, his control of temper, his family life and sex life, whether or not he drinks a great deal, and whether he has a gift of shepherding others humbly and tenderly.

7. *In the New Testament, they selected their leadership from men of experience*. No young man, no novice was considered. We ordain young men with no experience. We pay comparatively little attention to a candidate's morals. Provided he passes his college examinations he can be a drinker, bad tempered, greedy, taciturn and solitary: there is still room for him in the ordained ministry. The selectors do not even interview his wife and family, let alone discover whether or not he can manage his own household before being let loose on the household of God. And practically no attempt is made to find out whether or not the candidate enjoys a good reputation among unbelievers – something the early Christians found important.

This is of course because we see the ordained ministry as a career structure. Should we be doing anything of the sort? Is ministry much to do with books and memory, as we emphasise? Or is it more a matter of life and people, as the ancients thought? The question is at least worth asking. It affects training fundamentally.

8. *In the New Testament, men were trained on the job as apprentices, not in a college*. To be sure, colleges were not available to them. But college training did not come in until the nineteenth century. Was nobody properly trained until then? In the New Testament days, and for much of Christian history, men were trained on the job, in the fires of controversy, in the stress and strain of life. We take young men away from their natural milieu into semi-monastic institutions based on secular models, give them

book learning for three years, and wonder why they find it hard to fit in when we return them, not to their own area but to some quite different part of the country.

9. *In the New Testament, leaders were of two kinds, local and circulating.* The local ministry consisted of presbyters or bishops or shepherds (all, it seems, synonymous) assisted in administrative tasks by deacons, male and female. It might well contain men or women with outstanding gifts in prophecy, exorcism, healing or teaching. The circulating ministry would consist, in the early days, of the apostles and prophets moving round from place to place, evangelising, setting up churches, encouraging them and seeking to maintain their unity. Apostolic delegates like Timothy and Titus continued this role, which in the second century devolved upon the newly emerging monarchical bishops. But not only on them. We still find in the third and fourth centuries itinerant teachers, theologians, evangelists and prophets moving round the churches in an encouraging and supervisory function, enlarging horizons and preserving catholicity. It would appear that the effective combination of the settled and the mobile ministry might still have a great deal to offer the church.

10. *In New Testament days, local ministry consisted of people called to serve and lead in their own locality.* It did not consist of ministers from outside the community who came in for a spell of years and then departed. Once again it is not hard to see the value of the local man, well known and respected in his community, exercising the leadership of the local church in the company of other leaders, one or two of whom might well be from outside, so as to stimulate fresh ideas.

11. *In New Testament days, leaders were normally not paid.* They generally exercised a 'tent-making' ministry, thus solving at a stroke the financial problems that often today centre round the leadership of the churches. Of course, they might on occasion be paid: St. Paul contends eloquently in 1 Corinthians 9 for the principle that this

could be proper: but equally eloquently he makes it plain that he rarely availed himself of the privilege of being supported by the churches he came to serve.

12. *In the New Testament, the leaders saw theirs as an enabling ministry*. This is rare today. When an ordained man comes to a church he expects to do a great deal of the work. The congregation expect that he should. It is the exception, rather than the rule, to find him exercising a ministry of equipping the saints for the work of ministry, as Paul put it in Ephesians 4:12. The leader's task in the early church was not to do all the ministry himself, but to help other members of the Body of Christ to find out what their contribution to the service of the whole should be, and then do it.

13. *In the New Testament, doctrine was important*. Two qualities were looked for outside the character qualifications we have already glanced at. The candidate must be 'apt to teach' and must be noted for 'holding fast the faithful word'. He must be sound in the apostolic faith and competent in helping others to understand it and live by it. Nowadays, in contrast, one can be ordained in most denominations with the haziest notions about the existence of God, the deity of Christ, the role of scripture or the way of salvation. And men are ordained from some of the theological colleges without having ever preached a sermon under supervision, let alone having spoken on closed-circuit TV, or to a non-captive audience in the open air or taught in a school or on a factory floor. The ability to communicate is not rated highly in our training institutions. Is it any wonder that the common man regards the church as not for the likes of him?

14. *In the New Testament, ministry was seen in terms of people, not buildings*. Naturally, that is how we would all like it to be today. But the fact remains that many clergy are condemned to be the custodians of ancient buildings with insufficient resources for their upkeep. As a result, most of their effort inevitably goes into upkeep rather than

mission. The whole thrust of the ministry in the early church, when they had no buildings to maintain, was flexible and designed to build up congregations so that they could grow and spread the gospel elsewhere. Mission is nowadays in bondage to maintenance.

Of course it is proper to ask in what way we are entitled to turn to the New Testament for guidelines, so different were the men of the first century both historically and culturally from ourselves. We could not, even if we would, return to their situation. Their preoccupations – circumcision, meat offered to idols, and women's heads veiled in worship – are not ours. Not that those New Testament issues have nothing to teach us: they have. The abiding principles of equal acceptance of all believers before God, of refusal to compromise with evil, and of modesty, remain to guide us when the circumstances in which those principles found flesh and blood in New Testament days have faded away. But we should be foolish to look to the New Testament as a blueprint for 'the ministry'. For one thing, those pages tell a story of staggering diversity. Congregationalists, Presbyterians, Episcopalians, Brethren and Roman Catholics can all point to some element in ministry in the New Testament as justification for their own brand of ecclesiastical polity. Pentecostals can find all they need in Acts and 1 Corinthians, and Quakers can turn with some propriety to the Johannine corpus where no form of ordained ministry is apparently envisaged. For another thing, the New Testament does not give the impression that nothing should be done for the first time. On the contrary, most of the advances in definition of specific ministries recorded there seem to derive from the needs of the situation rather than from any preconceived normative plan; for instance, the appointment of the seven, often called 'deacons' in Acts 6, the initiatives of the first missionary journey in Acts 13, the appointment of presbyters in every city evangelised in that journey (Acts 14:23) and the establishment of the Apostolic Council in Acts 15.

No, if we are prepared to take the scriptures seriously as foundation documents of our faith, it does not mean that we shall follow them slavishly irrespective of context and

culture. But it does mean that we will face the challenges
and opportunities of our own generation with a good deal
more attention to the precedents afforded by church
history, and the principles and precepts of the New Testament from which we have so markedly turned away.

Let us begin at the fountain head, go back to Jesus
Christ, and see if he gives us any guidelines for Christian
ministry.

CHAPTER TWO

THE MODEL FOR MINISTRY

If there is one word to sum up the ministry of Jesus, it is this: service. His whole ministry was one of service. This is apparent from the general tenor of the Gospel narrative, and from many specific utterances. 'The Son of Man came not to be served but to serve, and to give his life as a ransom for many' he told his followers. As he took the way to the cross, he made it clear that service was to be the hallmark of all Christian ministry. In contrast to worldly rulers, pre-occupied with status and authority, 'It shall not', he said, 'be so among you; but whoever would be great among you must be your servant, and whoever would be first among you must be slave of all.' (Mark 10:43,44)

This lesson of the royalty of service must have been imprinted indelibly on the minds of the disciples by what happened at the Last Supper. In the Middle East feet quickly get hot and dusty, and it was the job of the household slave to wash them. At the Last Supper there was no household slave.

None of the apostles was willing to lose face by doing the slave's job; so they sat with unwashed feet. We can imagine the amazement when Jesus rose from supper and laid aside his garments. Wrapping a towel round his waist, he began to wash their feet (John 13:4,5). He was introducing them to a revolutionary idea of greatness — measured in terms of service. Relentlessly he pressed the point home. 'Do you know what I have done to you? You call me Teacher and Lord; and you are right, for so I am. If I then, your Lord and Teacher, have washed your feet, you

also ought to wash one another's feet. For I have given you
an example, that you also should do as I have done to you.
Truly, truly, I say to you, a servant is not greater than his
master; nor is he who is sent greater than he who sent him.
If you know these things, blessed are you if you do them.'
(John 13:12–17)

There is, I think, a hint in St. Luke's account that this
action of Jesus arose out of a quarrel among the disciples
over precedence and status. Although he does not record
the foot washing, Luke does tell us of this devastating
question which Jesus asked them at the meal: 'For which is
the greater, one who sits at table or one who serves? Is it
not the one who sits at table? But I am among you as one
who serves.' (Luke 22:27) Once more Jesus makes it crystal
clear that what is true of him must be true of his disciples.
'The kings of the Gentiles exercise lordship over them . . .
but not so with you; rather let the greatest among you
become as the youngest, and the leader as one who serves.'
(Luke 22:25,26)

The Christian church has found this a very hard lesson
to swallow. Almost all consideration of church unity
revolves round discussions on the validity of orders, their
regularity, their authentication and their apostolicity. That
is very natural. It is the way of the world. But it is not the
way of Jesus Christ. He saw ministry not in terms of status
but in terms of function. The pattern he set was the pattern
of service. Of course, the very word 'ministry' means
'service'. But for Jesus this was no idle euphemism. It is no
accident that the term 'ministry' is used to describe the
whole of his public life and work. He was supremely and in
everything the Servant of the Lord. That was his glory. He
looked for no other. And so it must be with any ministry
which claims to be truly Christian.

Jesus the Servant

How did Jesus come to think of himself in this light? He
found it in his Bible, particularly in Isaiah 40–55. Here it is
made very plain that the whole nation of Israel was called to
be the Servant of the Lord; service is the corollary of

election (Isa. 41:8–20). The particular elements of service which God looks for are obedience (Isa. 44:1; 65:12) witness (Isa. 43:12) and endurance (Isa. 43:1–6). But the nation refused to obey, recoiled from suffering and, instead of witnessing to the Lord, gave way to idolatry. And so the task of the Servant of the Lord devolved on a faithful remnant within Israel who accepted its implications. In the four Servant Songs of Isaiah (Isa. 42:1–4; 49:1–6; 50:4–7; 52:13–53:12) the great themes are obedience, witness and endurance. The Servant is utterly obedient to God's voice (Isa. 42:1; 50:4,5), witnesses both to the lapsed in Israel and to the Gentiles (Isa. 49:6) and suffers ignominy and pain (Isa. 50:5,6). Indeed, though innocent, he bears the sins of the people (Isa. 53:6,11,12) and God accepts his sacrifice and vindicates his cause (Isa. 53:10–12).

We may never know how the prophet thought his words would be fulfilled, but it is certain that Jesus saw in them the foreshadowing of his own ministry. At his baptism the voice from heaven addressed him as 'My beloved Son, with thee I am well pleased' (Mark 1:11). These words are a composite citation of Psalm 2:7 and Isaiah 42:1. Jesus, the messianic Son, is hailed as the Servant of the Lord in whom he is well pleased. The point is made equally emphatically at the outset of the fourth Gospel, where Jesus is greeted by the Baptist as 'the Lamb of God who takes away the sin of the world' (John 1:29,36). This title would, of course have taken the Jewish hearers back to the sacrificial system they knew so well. But it would have done more. It would have pointed the perceptive among them to the Suffering Servant of Isaiah 53, for *talya*, the Aramaic word for 'lamb' is also the word for 'servant'.

The three themes of utter obedience, fearless witness and innocent suffering, which marked the Old Testament understanding of the Servant, run through the ministry of Jesus. And so when at Caesarea Philippi Peter made his great confession that Jesus was the Messiah, the long-awaited deliverer of Jewish expectation, Jesus 'charged them to tell no one about him' (Mark 8:30). If they were thinking in terms of status and position they were entirely missing the point. So Jesus reinterpreted Peter's confession. He would not allow the term 'Christ' or 'Messiah' which suggested earthly pomp and military might. Instead, he joined together two utterly diverse concepts, and in effect asked Peter to see him in terms of them. 'He began to teach them that the *Son of Man* must *suffer* many things and be rejected.' Oscar Cullmann[1] was not exaggerating when he wrote:

> Son of Man represents the highest conceivable declaration of exaltation in Judaism; *ebed Yahweh* (the Servant of the Lord) is the expression of the deepest humiliation. This is the unheard-of new act of Jesus, that he united these two apparently contradictory tasks in his self-consciousness, and that he expressed that union in his life and teaching.

The concept of the Servant was never far from Jesus's mind, as can be seen by a whole page full of references and allusions gathered by Joachim Jeremias.[2] Moreover it clearly became the dominant theme towards the end of his ministry. By word and deed Jesus demonstrated that he was fulfilling the task of the Servant to the bitter end (Luke 22:37, John 13:4ff; Matt. 26:28). Peter understood this (1 Pet. 2:21ff) and so did Paul (Phil. 2:6,7). Both of them, in fact, make specific reference to Isaiah 53. Two of the early speeches in Acts refer to Jesus as God's Servant (Acts 3:13, 26; 4:27,30) and there are other New Testament allusions, such as Romans 15:7–12. Naturally, this title gave way to others, more comprehensive, after his resurrection, notably 'Lord': but it cannot be denied that the prevailing pattern and supreme glory of his ministry was service. It was, therefore, entirely in character when Jesus knelt to wash the disciples' feet. The Servant of the Lord had shrunk from the nation of Israel, from the faithful remnant, to a single person who fully embodied the vision. Later, that ministry was to expand again in his followers. Their ministry was to be marked by service.

The church of the Servant

Jesus is *the* Servant. He is *our* Servant. No man can be a

Christian, let alone a Christian minister, until he lets Jesus be his Servant. As we have seen, Peter rebelled against so humbling and embarrassing an encounter with Jesus the Servant. But he learnt his lesson, and his first Letter is full of the theme of the Servant. 'Submit' is the word that comes again and again; it is applied to husbands and wives, to young and old, to slaves – and to Christian leaders. In 1 Peter 5.5 he uses a rare word for '*Clothe yourselves*, all of you, with humility.' It recalls the way in which Jesus took a towel and girded himself. It is Peter's way of saying that the church must be like Jesus. It must be the church of the Servant. Christian life begins when we allow Jesus to be our Servant. It continues as, incorporated into Christ, we share the role of the Servant which he made so much his own. Of course we cannot share in the Servant's atoning work. He and he alone took responsibility for the sins of the world. But we can and must make his pattern of ministry our own. Indeed, he commissions us to do so. That is plain from the two mission charges to the twelve (Mark 6:7ff) and the seventy (Luke 10:1). We meet the same characteristics of service that we saw in Isaiah and in the life of Jesus. They are to obey the instructions of Jesus in going out on his mission. They are to bear witness to the kingdom of God by preaching, healing and casting out demons. And they are to be prepared for suffering and rejection. Their ministry is, in fact, an extension of their master's. It is conceived in the same terms, be it for the twelve or the seventy. For apostles and for church alike the pattern is the same. 'In the kingdom, service is not a stepping stone to nobility,' observed T. W. Manson:[3] 'it is nobility, the only kind of nobility that is recognised.'

   As the counterpart to this, Jesus warns his disciples against the preoccupation with status and succession that bedevilled the Jewish rabbinic schools. 'They love the place of honour at feasts, and the best seats in the synagogues, and salutations in the market places, and being called rabbi by men. But you are not to be called rabbi, for you have one teacher, and you are all brethren. And call no man your father on earth, for you have one Father who is in heaven. Neither be called masters, for you have one master, the

Christ. He who is greatest among you shall be your
servant.' (Matt. 23:6–11)

Such is the pattern for ministry set by Jesus. And he
was the one who 'taught them as one who had authority and
not as the scribes', the one to whom 'all authority in heaven
and on earth' had been committed (Mark 1:22; Matt.
28:18). It was the Christ, the Son of Man, the Son of God,
who took upon him the form of the Servant. He had
irrefragable credentials had he wished to rely on status and
authority. But he resolutely refused to countenance any
such suggestion. To him the authority of the Servant lay
simply in the fact of his service. The divine call, the divine
equipment by the Holy Spirit were demonstrated in a life of
obedience, witness and endurance. These, and not some
ecclesiastical counterpart to Gentile hierarchy or Jewish
succession (Luke 22:25; Matt. 23:7,8) were to be the
authenticating marks of Christian ministry.

When we reflect on the history of the church, are we
not bound to confess that she has all too often failed to
follow the model set by her founder? Frequently she has
worn the robes of the ruler, not the towel of the servant.
Even in our own day it can hardly be said that the brand
image of the church is a society united in love for Jesus and
devoted to selfless service of others.

If the whole church has failed, the ministry has failed
even more signally to exhibit the character of the Servant.
Even when we leave the past out of account, where pope
and pastor, bishop and minister, priest and synod have all
alike at times domineered over those in their charge instead
of being examples to the flock (1 Pet. 5:3), the present is
nothing to be proud about. Does the vicar give the
impression of being the servant of his people? Does he not
rather behave, as too often the missionary has behaved,
like a little tin god, loving to be recognised and looked up
to, anxious that nothing shall go on in the parish without his
personal supervision? Is it not an astonishing reversal of the
pattern left by Jesus when a bishop, a chief pastor in the
flock, revels in the title 'My Lord'? The whole gamut of
ecclesiastical titles, from 'Father' to 'Reverend', from
'Venerable' to 'Very Reverend' give quite the wrong

impression and distance their holders from the people they are called to serve.

Even today in the ecumenical scene, does the ministry seek to commend itself by the marks of the Servant, or are not the issues quite differently drawn up? When Rome insists on submission to the Roman pontiff as 'altogether necessary to salvation for every human creature' (the Bull *Unam Sanctam*) is this the way of Jesus?

The question is vital and urgent. It is a nettle that must be grasped. In today's world there is an increasing unwillingness to accept traditional or authoritarian pronouncements from any source on doctrine or ethics. In the ecumenical field, greater rapprochement is threatened by heavily entrenched doctrines of ministry which are quite uninfluenced by the example and teaching of Jesus. And in most parts of the developing world there is a continuing desire for help from the older churches, provided that such new-style missionaries come like their master 'not to be served, but to serve'. Unless more than lip service is paid to this pattern of the Servant in ministry, the prospects of advance in any of these three fields remain lamentably small.

CHAPTER THREE

A CHURCHFUL OF MINISTERS

Did the early church follow up the ideals of service laid down by Jesus? Or were they overwhelmed by the patterns of leadership all round them in pagan society?

Ministry for all Christians

The New Testament gives no suggestion that one could possibly be a Christian without at the same time being called to some ministry within the church. The Christian is indeed 'saved to serve'. St. Paul, for one, could never forget that the voice of the ascended Christ at his conversion had said: 'Rise and stand upon your feet; for I have appeared to you for this purpose, to appoint you *to serve and bear witness*' (Acts 26:16). It is hardly surprising, therefore, that the whole point of his argument in Romans 12 and 1 Corinthians 12 is that every member of the church has his or her part to play in the service of God. All without exception have a ministry.

Three words in particular are used to describe the devoted service of the person who knows himself to have been forgiven.

1. The first is *doulos*. It means, quite baldly, bondslave. And it comes a great many times in the New Testament. It was a word which Paul sometimes used to describe his relation to his converts (1 Cor. 9:19; 2 Cor. 4:5) but more often his relation to Jesus. He was 'the bondslave of Jesus Christ' (Rom. 1:1, etc.). He spoke of wearing the chain of

the slave, of being branded with the marks of the slave (2 Tim. 1:16; Gal. 6:17). He saw wholehearted dedication to Jesus as the only possible reaction of the redeemed. 'You are not your own; you were bought with a price,' he asserts (1 Cor. 6:19,20). Peter makes the same plea on the same grounds: 'You know that you were ransomed . . . with the precious blood of Christ' (1 Pet. 1:18,19), and he describes apostate Christians as 'denying the master who bought them' (2 Pet. 2:1).

This metaphor of the slave was particularly telling in the first century. The Roman slave belonged entirely to his master. He had no rights in law, and could demand no privileges. His money, his time, his future, his marriage were all, strictly speaking, at the disposal of his master. That is what it meant to be a slave. And that is the image that the New Testament writers deliberately took over.

But it was not applied only to the apostles or the leadership. To be sure, they are included; and Paul and Peter, James and Jude delight to call themselves the bond-slaves of Jesus (Jas. 1:1; Jude 1). But it is a characteristic description of all Christians without distinction (Rev. 1:1; 1 Pet. 2:16). Could anything show more graphically their loving devotion and total dedication to Christ? Should this not shame into silence our arguments about the status and validity of ministers? The highest ministry of all is open to all – to be bondslaves of Jesus Christ.

2. The second word used of Christian service is *leitourgos*, from which we get our word 'liturgy'. If *doulos* speaks particularly of Christian devotion to Christ, *leitourgos* speaks of Christian worship of God. This is the word used of angels in heaven and men on earth when they worship the Lord and surrender themselves in loving adoration to him (Heb. 1:14; Luke 1.23; Acts 13:2).

Sometimes the Jewish background of the term is uppermost, as in the Epistle to the Hebrews, where it is made very clear that the Old Testament priestly offerings, though ineffectual in themselves, are filled with meaning when seen in the light of Christ's work (Heb. 8:2; 10:11, 12).

On the other hand, Paul draws on the imagery of pagan worship when he calls the faith of the Philippians a 'liturgy' (Phil. 2:17). Christian giving is described in this way (2 Cor. 9:12; Rom. 15:27). It is the practical outworking of genuine worship of God. And for Epaphras to give himself, for the Lord's sake, to the service of Paul was no less worthy of the name (Phil. 2:30). When Paul preaches the gospel to the heathen, this too is *leitourgia* (Rom. 15:16) because through it the converts are' offered' to God. In short, this word speaks of the service of God in worship and work. It is brought before us as the right and duty of every Christian (even, in Romans 13:6, of a pagan magistrate exercising his responsibilities dutifully). In no way is it something which is restricted or delegated to any one class within the church.

3. The third and most common word to describe a minister is *diakonos*, from which our word 'deacon' is derived. It is, like the other two, applied to all and sundry within the church. Jesus and the apostles are called by this name: so are the humblest believers. It refers particularly to service of others, often menial service at that. The varieties of such service are vast. In Acts 6, for instance, the apostles were ministering the word of God to the people and the seven were administering famine relief. Both are styled *diakonia* (Acts 6:1–4). The New Testament does not follow our false distinction between the sacred and the secular. The whole of life is hallowed by God's creation, Christ's incarnation, and our conscious offering of all we do to him. The early church was well aware that it was called to carry on the work of the Servant.

We find the word *diakonia* used in 1 Corinthians 16:15 of what we would call church work. It is no less appropriate to the personal service rendered by Timothy and Erastus to Paul (Acts 19:22) – including, no doubt, taking down his letters, washing his clothes and cooking his meals. Prison visiting is given this honourable title in Philemon 13, and so is evangelistic preaching in Acts 20:24. Indeed, glancing through the Acts alone, you see the breadth of this term. It is applied to the ministry of feeding hungry people (Acts

6:1); the ministry of teaching hungry minds (Acts 6:4); the ministry of prayer (Acts 6:4); the ministry of giving to Christians in need in another country (Acts 11:29); the ministry of evangelism (Acts 21:19); the ministry of humble assistance as and when required (Acts 19:22); the ministry of living the whole of life for Christ even in the face of suffering and hardship (Acts 20:24). *Diakonia*, in short, belonged to the whole Church and to every member of it. No service was regarded as too menial or exacting if it would commend the gospel of the grace of God.

Emil Brunner[1] put it succinctly:

> One thing is supremely important; that *all* minister, and that nowhere is to be perceived a separation, or even merely a distinction, between those who do and those who do not minister, between the active and the passive members of the body, between those who give and those who receive. There exists in the *Ecclesia* a universal duty and right of service, a universal readiness to serve, and at the same time the greatest possible differentiation of functions.

Specialised ministries for some Christians

The fact that service is the hallmark of all Christians does not dispense with the need for specialisation within the Christian community. St. Paul sees the church as the Body of Christ, that is to say the agent of his purposes and bearer of his life in the world. Christians are like members within the human body; they have different functions, offer different types of service to the whole body, and are alike under the unified direction of the head.

Romans 12:4–8 urges Christians to discover and make the most of their God-given abilities for the good of the whole. Paul mentions the *charismata* (love-gifts from God) of prophecy, helpful service, teaching, encouragement, giving, leadership and pastoral concern as examples of what he means; and love is the bond which unites these diverse gifts into the harmonious unity of the Body. The function of leadership within the church is just one of the many gifts of God to his people.

I Corinthians 12 uses the same metaphor, and makes the added point that this differentiation of function within the Body is a sovereign act of God the holy Trinity (v.4–6). The church is seen as a living organism in which God gives different tasks for each member to embody. Indeed, the contributions of various parts to the whole are described in this passage by four interesting words. They are *pneumatica*, functions assigned by the Holy Spirit. They are *charismata*, gracious enduements by God for service. They are *energemata*, a word which suggests the power in which these gifts are to be exercised. They are *diakoniai*, different types of service to and in the Body. Paul concludes the chapter by applying all this to a variety of ministries within the Corinthian church. They fall roughly into four groupings: ministry of the word ('first apostles, second prophets, third teachers); ministry of healing ('then workers of miracles, then healers'); ministry of leadership and administration ('helpers, helmsmen' – what a superbly illuminating title for Christian leadership!); and finally the ministry the Corinthians (wrongly) prized the most, 'speakers in various kinds of tongues' and their interpretation. God's purpose is that by mutual caring each member should use his gift for the good of the whole Body.

Ephesians 4:8–13 underlines this theme. Paul is speaking of the gifts of the ascended Christ to his church: 'and his gifts were that some should be apostles, some prophets, some evangelists, some pastors and teachers, for the equipment of the saints for the work of ministry, for building up the body of Christ'. That is a lovely description of the leaders of a church. They do not lord it over the congregation. They are not hired and fired at the whim of the congregation. They are a team. They are the farewell gift of the ascended Christ to that congregation, and their special task is to build up the members for their work of service.

It can hardly be accidental that each of the ministries mentioned here is a ministry of the word. They exist within the Body to equip the church to play its part in the world.

In his book *Let My People Grow*[2] Michael Harper has given considerable care to studying these five ministries of apostle, prophet, evangelist, shepherd and teacher. He argues most convincingly that all five represent facets of ministry in any healthy church.

We need the apostolic deposit in scripture and the circulating, supervising role which is now embodied in bishops and travelling teachers.

Equally we need the prophetic ministry. It belonged to the foundation layer of the church (Eph. 2:20; 3:5) and it has not died out. God still guides his people through prophecy, that is, a word from himself directly applicable to the situation of that church. As early as the *Didache* at the end of the first century it was necessary to test prophecy carefully: credulity is no Christian virtue. Thus 'No prophet who orders a meal while "in the Spirit" shall eat of it; otherwise he is a false prophet.' (11.7) Very shrewd advice! But none the less the *Didache* has the highest respect for the genuine prophet. Abuse does not abolish use, and one of the crying needs in the contemporary church is the recovery of the prophetic gift.

Every church needs evangelists. These may or may not be ordained people. It is the gift that is needed, not the ordination! A church that does not evangelise will slowly die. And if it has nobody in it with an evangelistic gift, that aspect of its ministry to the world around is likely to atrophy. All Christians are called to witness to Christ. But some Christians have a special gift of evangelism, and this gift is to be valued and used in the congregation.

Pastors are no less vital. People need caring for. Troubles need to be spilled out and problems shared. In every congregation there are those who have gifts in this direction. They constitute a priceless part of the leadership of the church, an invaluable gift from the ascended Christ for the benefit of his Body.

Finally, teachers are indispensable. Probably these are the same as the 'teachers' of 1 Corinthians 12:28 and the presbyter-bishops of Acts 20 and the Pastoral Epistles: in both places great emphasis is placed on their teaching the word of God (Acts 20:24–32, 1 Tim. 3:2, Titus 1:9). This teaching function, we are told (Eph. 4:11,12) is the supreme task of what we would call the ordained ministry, that is the part of the Body expressly charged with the duty of equipping the 'saints' for their service in the world.

Now surely this is a very remarkable thing. We tend to assume today that the purpose of the clergy is primarily to do with leading public worship and celebrating the sacraments. These functions are never once attributed to the ordained ministry in the New Testament! The ministry there is first and foremost concerned with *didache*, the teaching of Christians so that they may more effectively be the church in the world. That is to say, ministry exists for the sake of the church (and not vice versa, as is so often either taught or implied), just as the church in her turn exists for the sake of the world. The pattern of the Servant remains.

Clergy and laity?

One of the most firmly held assumptions in any of the mainline churches is that there is a clear distinction between clergy or ministers and laymen. Christianity is like a train with two classes of passenger in it. The clergy are the first-class passengers in this particular train. They are the professionals, and the laymen the amateurs; they are the priests, and the laymen the people.

All this would have sounded very strange to New Testament ears. They knew nothing of any such distinction! And this is all the more amazing when you recall that every society in the world, including Israel, had its specialised holy seasons, holy places and holy people. In Christianity all three were abolished – or rather universalised. The keeping of holy days was a matter of indifference to the early Christians (Rom. 14:5,6). They had no holy buildings, but met in private houses (e.g. Rom. 16:23): the incarnation had made the secular sacred. As to holy people, why, all believers were called to be that holy people, that universal priesthood envisaged long ago in the Old Testament but never hitherto realised (1 Pet. 2:5). The mediation of Jesus had abolished the need for an intermediary caste of priests. All can have access to God by virtue of his sacrifice. All are charged with the priestly responsibility of interceding for men to God. There is no priestly body within Christianity. It is a one-class society, though you would never guess as much, so grossly has conformity to pagan and Old Testament models distorted this unique facet of Christ's community. Although not all men are called to the function of Christian leadership, the church remains a one-class society. There is no suggestion to be found within the New Testament of what subsequently developed into the disastrous two-class system of clergy and laity.

The etymology of the two words is interesting and their usage suggestive. Clergy derives from *kleros*, God's lot or heritage. Laity comes from *laos*, the people of God. These words are not contrasted in the New Testament. *All* Christians constitute God's *kleros* (Acts 26:18; Col. 1:12 and supremely 1 Pet. 5:3 where the word is used of what we would call the laity!). *All* Christians, equally, go to make up God's *laos* (2 Cor. 6:16; 1 Pet. 2:9,10). Just as the distinction between those who do and those who do not minister is abolished in Christ, so is the age-old divide between the professional man of God and the amateur, the cleric and the layman. The Church belongs to the new age, the age of the kingdom of God, in which distinctions of status are done away with. So in the New Testament you do not find two standards of behaviour, one for the specially holy professional people and one for the ordinary Christians. The New Testament knows nothing of a priestly caste within the church. As J. B. Lightfoot put it in his celebrated *Essay on The Christian Ministry* 'the Christian ideal is a holy season extending the whole year round, a temple confined only by the limits of the habitable world, and a priesthood coextensive with the human race.'[3] Of course, the early Christians did not for that reason forego efficiency and organisation. To be sure, certain people generally led the services, which normally took place in this or that house. But this did not compromise the principle of the one-class society. Hear Lightfoot again:

For communicating instruction and for preserving public order, for conducting public worship and dispensing social charities, it became necessary to appoint special

officers. They are called stewards of God, servants or
ministers of the church, and the like; but the sacerdotal
title is never once conferred upon them. The only priests
under the gospel, designated as such in the New Testament, are the saints, the members of the Christian
brotherhood (1 Pet. 2:5,9; Rev. 1:6; 5:10; 20:6)[4]

That is why there is no hard and fast distinction
between clergy and laymen in the New Testament. All
alike are the servants and ministers of God. The New
Testament offers us a churchful of ministers!

CHAPTER FOUR

FAREWELL GIFT

One has only to voice the sentiments conveyed in the last chapter to be accused of having a low view of the ordained ministry. Actually, nothing could be further from the truth. If we take seriously the teaching we have just examined in Ephesians 4:7–16, we are driven to a very high doctrine of the ordained ministry.

But let us first of all exclude two contrasting errors which prevent us having a balanced perception of what the ordained ministry is and what it is meant to achieve. We need to avoid the twin but opposite errors of clericalism and anti-clericalism, of prelacy and anarchy, which equally stand condemned in the light of the New Testament.

Two contrasting errors

There is a tendency in some circles, and by no means only 'Catholic' ones, for the ordained minister to lord it over the flock committed to him. Nothing of any importance in the church can be done if he is not there. The wishes of the people in matters as widely different as ritual or policy are subordinated to his own. I have known parishes where the parochial council or vestry does not even exercise its statutory say in the finances of the church; they are administered entirely by the rector. I know of others where the parish priest does not even allow meetings for Bible reading and prayer to take place in private homes unless he is present. These are extreme, but by no means isolated examples of the danger of overvaluing the office of the ordained man. It is bad for the clergyman in such a situation; bad too for the congregation. It gives the former an exaggerated view of his own importance in the Body, and hinders the initiative and ministries of the latter. Wherever the principle of Romans 12, of diversity in unity, is forgotten, the church suffers. When one member exceeds his place, the whole Body is impoverished.

Equally dangerous, and scarcely less widespread, is a tendency to disparage the ordained ministry. This has, of course, sprung up as a reaction against long years of clerical domination. Some Christians, notably the Brethren, have no ordained ministry at all. Others interpret the priesthood of all believers as though it meant the priesthood of no believers. Others, as B. L. Manning once warned the Congregationalists, fall into the mistake of regarding the sacred ministry as a 'secretaryship, a sort of general manager's job, a device to save trouble for the majority of the church members by concentrating nearly all their duties upon one or two.'[1] This is to forget that the minister is not merely the servant of the church but the servant of Christ. It is from Christ that he derives his authority, and it is to Christ that he owes his allegiance. During his earthly life Jesus took great pains to train those whom he later commissioned as his apostles. After his resurrection he continued to 'give' ministers to his people (Eph. 4:11). There are those who 'bear rule' in the Christian churches (Heb. 13:7, 1 Thess. 5:12, 1 Tim. 5:17) and consequently there are those who are ruled. The church is not a democracy. The ordained ministry combines both the dignity and the lowliness of Jesus who commissions it.

For the truth lies neither with clericalism nor anticlericalism. The key to a right understanding is to realise that the ordained ministry is a parting gift of the ascended Christ. 'When he ascended on high he led a host of captives and he gave gifts to men.' What were these gifts? No less than the ordained ministry! 'His gifts were that some should be apostles, some prophets, some evangelists, some pastors and teachers, for the equipment of the saints for the work of ministry, for building up the Body of Christ.' (Eph. 4:8,11,12). Had you ever thought of the local minister as

God's gift to the church? That is what he is meant to be. Then you will neither undervalue him as if he were nothing, nor overvalue him as if nothing could happen without him. He is a gift to the Body.

And what is he for? This is a topic of widespread uncertainty these days. No longer is the clergyman the best-educated member of society. No longer is he the main teaching influence or caring agency. He is not even any longer a community leader. Then what is he for? For taking services or validating sacraments, or burying, baptising and marrying? No. He is for building up the saints for their work of service. He is, as it were, a petrol-pump attendant to get other cars mobile. He is an enabler of other men and women. That is what he is for.

And he does not stand alone. We have already seen in Chapter One that the ministry in early days was a shared one. We shall have occasion to look further into that, since the exposure, the loneliness and the autocracy of the one-man-ministry is a great factor in the current disenchantment with the church. This very passage specifies no less than five types of ministry which are designated as Christ's gift to the church: not one type – let alone one man in whom all the gifts are supposed to be combined by the wave of a hand at ordination! No, ministry should always be shared. That complementarity in unity is one of the aspects of God himself which he intends to see reproduced in the leadership of his people. It is not good for man to be alone in ministry any more than it is in marriage. The gift of God is not a clergyman, but a partnership of ministry.

So the leadership in a church is called to be neither complaisant nor authoritarian. They must be first and foremost servants of the Lord and then of the people they are called to serve; dedicated to the task of bringing them to Christian maturity, anxious to ensure that every part of the Body is working properly, so that the whole Body can be effective in representing Christ to a sceptical world. Only in such an extension of the work of the Servant can the true balance between the authority and the lowliness of the ordained ministry be preserved.

What is ordination?

We have been speaking all this time about the ordained ministry as if everyone knew what it was. Instead, it is a matter for sharp debate. It is clear from the New Testament that leaders were identifiable and diverse. We have already seen five types of leadership mentioned in Ephesians. If we look in New Testament ordination for a specific setting aside of three orders of ministry, bishops, priests and deacons, we shall look in vain. But if we ask whether the leadership, diverse as it undoubtedly was, was set aside specifically for the task with prayer, fasting and the imposition of hands, we shall find that this was the case. ,

In Acts 14:23 we read that Paul and Barnabas appointed 'elders' or 'presbyters' (it is the same word in Greek) in every church they had brought into being during the first missionary journey. The word used is *cheirotoneo*, which in later ecclesiastical usage means to impose hands in ordination. However, in secular usage the word simply means to 'choose' or 'appoint' (in Greek city-states the people originally exercised their choice by raising their hands). Such is the meaning of the word in its only other appearance in the New Testament, (2 Cor. 8:19), and in its three occurrences in Ignatius (*Philad.* 10.1, *Smyrn.* 11.2, *Poly.* 7.2), so you cannot be absolutely sure that Paul and Barnabas laid hands on these men to ordain them. In Acts 6 it is uncertain whether the apostles or the people lay hands on the seven; in any case it is not clear whether this is an ordination or an *ad hoc* measure to relieve a particular situation. The only other evidence from the New Testament concerns Timothy. Paul speaks of 'the gift of God which is within you through the laying on of my hands' (2 Tim. 1:6). This may refer to Timothy's ordination. It may equally indicate his baptism which was in those days accompanied by the laying on of hands (Heb. 6:1,2, Acts 9:17). If so, the only certain reference to ordination in the New Testament would be 1 Timothy 4:14. This may be translated with the R.S.V., 'Do not neglect the gift you have, which was given you by prophetic utterance when the elders laid their hands upon you.' Or it may mean, as

Daube[2] and Jeremias[3] have suggested 'when hands were laid upon you with the object of making you a presbyter.' Whichever is right, we see a primitive example of the solemn imposition of hands commissioning a man for ministry by those who were recognised as competent authorities in the church. These might be either an apostle (as perhaps in the case of Timothy) or an apostolic delegate (see Titus 1:5 and ?1 Tim. 5:22) or those who were already elders (?1 Tim. 4:14). There would thus be a public recognition by the Body of Christ of the gift of leadership imparted by God to a particular member; and a commissioning of him, through their representatives, to exercise that gift for the benefit of the Body as a whole. In that sense, and in that sense alone, is there any difference between clergy and laymen in the New Testament.

Coming to the modern church, the question 'What is ordination?' can be answered at two levels.

At the organisational level the answer in most churches is unambiguously clear. It is seen in terms of status and authorisation. In the Anglican Church, to which I belong, it is the authorisation by the bishop to pronounce the absolution, to preach the Word of God, and to administer the sacraments.

But what is ordination at a deeper and theological level? It is the 'setting apart, because of God's calling, of those who exercise a ministry of the Word logically prior to other ministries, which enables the church to develop into the pure Body of Christ.'[4] It is 'a call to the service of leadership, addressed publicly to a believer, by which the church sanctions the call of God.'[5] The essential theological point has been clearly grasped by Michael Harper[6]: 'Ordination is essentially a recognition of abilities already evidenced in the life of a person and the authorisation of that person to exercise his gifts in the Body of Christ.' There need be no battle between charism and office in the church so long as ordination is the public recognition by the people of God of the charism of leadership already evidenced, at least germinally, in the candidates.

If, then, we look for a setting aside of ministers by prayer and the imposition of hands, there is clear evidence for it in the New Testament. If we construe this ministry too narrowly, we shall go wrong. Presbyter-bishops, apostolic delegates, deacons and deaconesses, prophets and prophetesses, evangelists, pastors and teachers all qualify as that enabling ministry through which the rest of the Body is edified. Does this not suggest that our concept of ordination might usefully be broadened?

Would it be too radical to suggest that the way in which the ministry of various members in local churches in deprived areas as well as flourishing ones, could best be furthered would be by the bishop (or other competent authority) setting apart with prayer and the laying on of hands those within the congregation who display the *charism* of leadership? This would, after all, merely be an extension of the representative idea that the whole people of God may, as a matter of order, be represented by a person authorised to act in the name of the congregation – a principle which underlies 'ordination' as we know it at present. Such people need not attend a theological college provided that they were carefully trained on the job, supervised and encouraged. They would earn their bread and butter from a secular calling, but their supreme concern would be for the building up of Christ's people. It might be proper to restrict their leadership to the local community where they live – they might not necessarily be called to the same role if they moved to another community. The important thing is that by recognising those who have the God-given charism of leadership in the church (which may well be displayed by those who are by no means natural leaders in secular life) we would be following an important New Testament principle of recognising and ordaining tried local leaders. In this way money would be saved, and the unedifying practice of churches being herded together into a Group or Team irrespective of pastoral considerations would be avoided. So would the ridiculous expedient of one 'ordained' man running around half a dozen churches administering Holy Communion, just because they have not got their own 'minister'.

Ordained and other ministries

It is clear that all Christians are called to serve. It is also clear from the New Testament that some Christians are charged with a ministry of the word and of leadership which is a facilitating ministry and is logically prior to other ministries within the Body of Christ. Does this mean that there should be inviolable separate spheres for 'clergy' and 'laymen'? We have already looked at this in principle, and seen that there is no theological justification for it. But let us look now at three areas normally restricted to the 'clergy' and see how the principle might work out in practice.

1. *Teaching the faith* is an important function of the specialised ministry. And yet in the Corinthian church there was room for any member to take part in the ministry of the word if he or she had something to contribute (1 Cor. 14:26–29). Indeed, the fact that any member of the congregation may speak out for the Lord is what powerfully convinces the unbeliever coming in that God is in their midst (1 Cor. 14:24, 25). Clearly, then, while teaching is the special function of what we might call the 'ordained ministry' it is not exclusively theirs. I see no reason why men and women in our congregations should not teach the faith in the collegiality of leadership which goes to make up a healthy church.

2. *Leading in worship* may well have been a function of the 'ordained ministry' (though we are not expressly told so); but there is no indication that it should be restricted to them. On the contrary, any member of the congregation was free to contribute his teaching, his prophetic utterance or picture, his hymn or psalm, even his contribution in tongues, provided it was interpreted, so that the Body could be edified (1 Cor. 14:26ff). For centuries the element of *risk* in vital corporate worship of this kind has seemed too great: there is very little danger of disorder arising from excessive congregational participation in the older established churches of the world!

In some of the younger churches that risk is being taken, and is being justified. The growth of Pentecostal churches (and charismatic congregations within the older denominations) is one of the undeniable features in the religious life of our day. This growth may be due to many causes, but high among them must feature the large extent of lay participation. Every Christian among them sees it as his duty and privilege to take part in the leading of worship as and when appropriate, and to bear witness to Christ in his home, at work or in the open air when that is called for. The saints have been equipped, in however inadequate a way, for service; and they grow in spiritual effectiveness, joy and commitment because they are actually involved rather than being, as in many a church, almost an audience of spectators. There can be no justification for restricting the leadership in worship to the clergy exclusively.

3. A third area which, above all, has been associated with the clergy alone is *the celebration of the sacraments*. It is significant that in the New Testament we are never told who should baptise and who should preside at the Communion. It apparently never occurred to the first generation of Christians that these actions hung together as a specific area into which no 'layman' might trespass. The word 'sacrament' is never found in the New Testament. It is derived from the heathen world of the Graeco-Roman society, and although it is none the worse for that, it seems to have brought pagan ideas over with it. There is a good deal of truth in Emil Brunner's contention[7] that with Ignatius' emphasis early in the second century on the Eucharist as the *pharmakon athanasias* 'the medicine of immortality' and the bishop as the only distributor of it (*Ephes.* 20.2) we have passed from the New Testament conception of the church as a unity of persons redeemed by Christ and united in the Spirit, to an idea of the church as a collective whose unity flows from their common relationship to a thing, the sacrament. Be that as it may, it seems reasonably clear that in the New Testament anyone can baptise. As Eduard Schweizer put it[8]: 'The apostles do not as a rule baptise (Acts 10:48, cf. 19:5 beside 6a, 1 Cor.

1:14–17). Ordinary church members do (Acts 9:18).' An overstatement no doubt, but the point is made!

It seems likely, too, that any suitably respected leader could preside at the Lord's Supper in the early days of the church. When Paul had to rebuke abuses in the church at Corinth there is no one individual he can blame. And if in Acts 2.46 the 'breaking bread from house to house' refers to the Eucharist, as it probably does, then that settles the matter. It is expressly stated that this is what the *converts* did. It was a lay celebration. In the Pastoral Epistles Paul expresses great concern over church order, but he never suggests that the celebration of the Eucharist or baptism is a function peculiar either to the presbyter-bishops whom Timothy and Titus are to ordain, or to the apostolic delegates themselves. Even as late as Justin in the middle of the second century (1 *Apology*, 65) we find the celebrant simply referred to as *ho prohestōs* 'the president', presumably because, as in the *Didache*, it is not yet invariably the task of one particular official.

I am not in the least advocating ecclesiastical anarchy. I am just seeking to separate principle from long-established custom. The principle is that Christianity knows of no special priestly cadre within Christ's priestly Body, the church. All Christians, not some, are called to minister. And this ministry will be as diverse as that of the various limbs in a human body. It is perfectly right and proper that certain people should normally carry out certain functions. What is wrong is to insist that nobody else can possibly carry them out even in an emergency. Thus in England there is normally no reason why 'laymen' should celebrate the Communion: there are enough ordained people to do so, at least in most parts of the land. But this is not the case in many missionary situations. On average eight women offer as missionaries to every one man. They frequently act as pioneers in the evangelisation of primitive tribes in places like New Guinea and Colombia. They administer the first baptisms and Communions, handing over to the local believers as soon as possible. Are we to stay in the comfort of our Western ivory towers and proclaim such ministries invalid? We may do so if we wish.

But we shall find no warrant in the New Testament for our position. There we are not presented with a hierarchy of ministers but a body of co-operating members, exercising their God-given gifts and functions for the good of the whole, as they carry out the work of the Servant in the world. All ministry is an act of God himself, and an essential part of ministry in the New Testament is that *an unqualified person* is called to it, in order 'to show that the transcendent power belongs to God and not to us' (2 Cor. 4:7).

Soon after New Testament days, however, a development set in which changed the Christian organism with its dynamic ministries into an organisation with institutionalised offices. When Paul wrote to the Corinthians he urged them to submit to their leaders in recognition of the quality of their service (1 Cor. 16:15,16). When Clement of Rome wrote to the Corinthians, less than half a century later, he urged them to reinstate their deposed presbyters because they had been properly appointed (1 *Clement* 44). The Christian fellowship had begun to give way to the ecclesiastical institution. The dynamic view of ministry had begun to give way to the static view of 'office'. The servant had begun to savour of the master. This is a process which we in our day should seek to reverse.

CHAPTER FIVE

THREEFOLD MINISTRY?

The Preface to the Anglican Ordinal asserts roundly, 'It is evident unto all men diligently reading the Holy Scriptures and Ancient Authors that from the Apostles' time there have been these Orders of Ministers in Christ's Church: Bishops, Priests and Deacons.' This statement is widely misquoted. It does not say 'there have been *three* Orders' that is, three only. It is not in the least polemical. The Reformers who framed the statement did not wish to unchurch their colleagues on the continent who had a different, perhaps presbyterian form of church government.

The views of the Reformers are well known. They agreed that all necessary doctrine was set forth in Holy Scripture: and the importance of episcopal ordination was not plainly set forth there. Thus Cranmer could say, 'I do not set more by any title, name or style than I do by the paring of an apple, further than that it shall be to the setting forth of God's word and will,'[1] and Bishop Hooper could write, 'I believe the church is bound to no sort of ministers or any ordinary succession of bishops . . . but only unto the Word of God[2]. Article XIX sets out the marks of the church: it does not indicate that any particular form of church government is necessary. It gives, on the contrary, precisely the same marks of the visible church as are laid down in the Reformed Continental Confessions of Saxony, Augsburg and Switzerland.

What the Preface was concerned to maintain is that the Church of England, in retaining at the Reformation the catholic orders of bishop, priest and deacon, did so because they saw those orders to be agreeable both to history and to scripture. It was a principle with Cranmer in his reforming work in England to retain what of 'the old may be well used'. His judgment cannot be faulted on biblical or historical grounds. You do not only find these three titles in scripture; you also find there a threefold division of ministry – the supervisory and circulating ministry, the local and settled ministry and the assistant ministry of the deacons.

If we look at the matter historically the same conclusion is reached. Nowhere do we find a 'parity of ministers'. Everywhere we encounter gradations of offices in the church. The threefold ministry was an established fact in the Asiatic churches at the end of the apostolic period as the writings of Polycarp and Ignatius make plain. By the middle of the second century the threefold ministry of bishop, priest, and deacon was the normal, almost universal pattern for Christian ministry the world over.

On the other hand, we must remember that other orders of ministry continued. Apostles, in the sense of wandering Christian leaders with a charismatic flavour, are highly regarded in the *Didache* and Ignatius. There were still prophets and prophetesses, still exorcists and miraculous healers. Witnesses as far apart as Justin in Rome (*Dial.* 38,82), Irenaeus in Gaul (*A.H.* 2.32.4,5), and Tertullian in North Africa (*de Anima* 9) not only attest their presence but regard them as part of God's ministerial gift to his church. In the Roman Church of the mid third century we find a fascinating catalogue of ministries: 46 presbyters, 7 deacons, 7 sub-deacons, 42 acolytes, and 52 exorcists, doorkeepers and readers (Eusebius *H.E.* 6.43). As a matter of fact Rome has showed more flexibility on varieties in ministry than many other churches. Jerome and Aquinas, for example, both refused to regard bishops as a different order from priests, and the Council of Trent defined that the two differed in *gradus* but not in *ordo*. It would be precarious, therefore, to interpret the Anglican Ordinal in any exclusive sense. This can easily be proved, if proof were needed, by the fact that in the sixteenth and seventeenth centuries the Church of England enjoyed the closest of ties (including intercommunion and occasional interchange of ministers), with her sister churches of the Reformation on the continent who had not retained the threefold ministry. What we may maintain with confidence is that the threefold ministry is securely grounded in both scripture and history; and so, without prejudice to other ministries, we shall proceed to examine those of bishop, priest and deacon.

Priest or presbyter

Their derivation

As we shall see later on, the Christian priest has nothing to do with the sacrificing priesthood of the Old Testament. The word is derived both historically and linguistically from the 'presbyter' or 'elder' of the New Testament.

But where did the idea come from? The answer is the Jewish synagogue. Any ten Jews could band together to form a synagogue, so it is hardly surprising that in Jewish areas 'Christian congregations were long called synagogues (Jas. 2:2). The civil and administrative duties of the synagogue devolved upon a board of presbyters, who saw that the law was observed, administered taxes, and, if necessary, enforced excommunication. They had no liturgical functions: these lay in the hands of the 'ruler of the synagogue'. He was not a priest of the Aaronic line, but, like the presbyters, he was a layman elected for the office.

Such was the model conveniently to hand for the new movement. The Christians took it over and adapted it. We find Christian presbyters all over the Mediterranean basin (Acts 20:17, 14:23, 1 Pet. 5:1 cf. 1:1, Jas. 5:14). We even find them figuring prominently in John's vision of heaven, where the four and twenty elders, representing Old and New Covenants, worship God continually (Rev. 4:4).

If this is so, why do we find no mention of presbyters in Paul's letters apart from the Pastoral Epistles? Chance may have something to do with it: we would have no mention of bishops either if Philippians had not been preserved. But it seems probable that the *presbyters* (or elders) were called *bishops* (or overseers) in Gentile churches, for that word was commonly used to denote any sort of supervision in the Graeco-Roman world. Thus at Philippi, in Asia Minor, and in Crete the presbyter is styled 'bishop' (Phil. 1:1, Acts 20:28, I Pet. 5:2, Titus 1:7). As we shall see, the two offices were the same, and it was merely a difference of nomenclature, and it was never uniform: 'bishop' never entirely eclipsed 'presbyter' even among Gentile congregations (1 Tim. 5:17, 1 Clem. 21.44).

Furthermore there was a broad variety of expression in the New Testament and particularly among the Pauline circle, to denote the ministerial office. The function is so much more important than the name. We are probably right in identifying the 'leader' of Hebrews 13:7,17, and the 'man who bears rule' (1 Thess. 5:12,13) with the presbyter. And the 'helps and leaderships' of 1 Cor. 12:28 are two divine gifts which soon crystallised into the diaconate and presbyterate respectively.

Their work

The most interesting of these names is 'those who bear rule'. The *proistamenos* (and its cognate form, *prostatēs*) originally denoted the powerful Roman 'patron' who had his 'clients'. The word then came to be applied to any person of wealth and influence who used his position to benefit the less fortunate. Clement of Rome once called Jesus 'the patron of our weakness' (36.1). The word sheds a fine light on the nature of Christian leadership. It is no doubt because of her championing the cause of her poorer and less influential Christian friends that Phoebe, the deaconess of the church of Cenchreae, is given this lovely title (Rom. 16.2).

These varied titles give some idea of the task of the ordained man. He is, first and foremost, a *presbyter*. The word means primarily a senior person, an elderly man. In some of the New Testament references (e.g. 1 Tim. 5:1–3, 17; 1 Pet. 5:1–5) it is notoriously hard to know whether

age or office is meant. Clearly young men were not
ordained: and one was generally considered a young man in
both Greek and Hebrew culture until the age of forty.

Then the title *bishop* describes the main function of
these elders. They are to supervise and oversee the congregations committed to them (Acts 20:28, 1 Pet. 5:2).
Presbyters, or senior people is what they *are*: bishoping or
oversight is what they *do*. This oversight will mean that
they are *pastors* to the congregation and are also *leaders* in
the church, not least, no doubt, in public worship. They are
to act like *patron* to client: this will involve material assistance for the needy, and admonition of the unruly (1 Thess.
5:12) along with support for the weak (Acts 20:35). Theirs
is supremely a *teaching* office, and this grew more
important as the church spread and the apostles died off.

Thus their work is in some ways parallel to and in some
ways much wider than that of the Jewish elder. Both bear
rule, both administer, both excommunicate (this is hinted
at in 1 Cor. 5:4,5). But unlike the Jewish elder the Christian
minister has a pastoral and probably a liturgical function as
well. Unlike them he is a teacher, and is entrusted with a
special ministry of prayer (Jas. 5:14). Perhaps the biggest
difference was this: all Christian rule was marked with the
imprint of Jesus the Servant. He had both told them and
shown them that the leader (*hegoumenos*) among them was
to adopt the role of the servant (*diakonos*). How could they
ever forget, when they used this title *hegoumenos* of
Christian presbyters, that its supremacy was one of service?
How could they ever be domineering over the flock in their
work as bishops, so long as they kept before their eyes the
oversight of Jesus, the bishop of their souls? (1 Pet. 5:3,
2:25).

A corporate and settled ministry

Two other points of some significance emerge from the
rather sparse evidence of the New Testament on presbyters. The first is that they represent a corporate and
settled ministry. The second is that there are not two types
of presbyter.

The presbyters were the local ministers of the church, in contrast to itinerant apostles, prophets and evangelists. This comes out particularly clearly in the Jerusalem church where, in the absence of the apostles on missionary journeys we read simply of 'the presbyters' or 'James and the presbyters' (Acts 11:30, 21:18). And, like their Jewish prototypes, they always appear in the plural throughout all the variety of titles used to describe them. They represent a collegiality of leadership, in striking contrast to most of their successors the world over. This is one of the areas where we most need to recapture the insight of the first Christians. At first it looks as if 1 Tim. 3:2 and Titus 1:7 are exceptions to this collegiality, but in fact this is not so. Paul tells his lieutenant Titus to ordain 'presbyters in every city . . . if any be blameless . . . for a bishop must be blameless.' In other words the singular, 'the bishop' is a generalising singular; the presbyters and the bishop are one and the same here as they are in the rest of the New Testament. Presbyters point us to the need for a fellowship of leadership in the church.

The Presbyterian Churches have been better than most of the rest of us in retaining this corporate leadership. But they have often made a sharp division between 'ruling elders' and 'teaching elders', following Calvin in Book 4 of the *Institutes*. The question turns on the interpretation of 1 Tim. 5:17 'Let the elders who rule well be considered worthy of double honour (or *pay*), especially those who labour in preaching and teaching.' There can be little doubt that all elders 'rule'. It seems to be implied, though, that not all elders labour at preaching and teaching. So does this mean there is an élite within the presbyteral board which spends itself in preaching and teaching? There is no suggestion elsewhere in the New Testament that this is so: many Presbyterians no longer hold it; and J. B. Lightfoot[3] plausibly interprets the verse as meaning 'as each has his special gift, so would he devote himself more or less exclusively to the one or the other of these sacred functions.' As one who has worked in such a team of presbyters for ten years I can only say that that is how in fact it works. There is one leadership group, but members within it have different and complementary gifts: that is what makes group leadership so important and so valuable for the church.

On any showing, the presbyterate in the early church showed a far more corporate oversight than most modern churches. The virtual autocracy of many a parish priest or nonconformist minister today is good neither for him nor for the congregation; it is clearly at variance with the pattern of Christian leadership in the New Testament; and it obscures the portrait of the Servant.

Bishops

Presbyter-bishops

In the New Testament bishops and presbyters or priests are the same. This, as Lightfoot showed, is the plain meaning of the texts, and his view is universally accepted nowadays.

The evidence for this identification of bishop and presbyter is as follows. In Acts 20 the elders of v.17 (*presbyteroi*) are called to exercise the function of bishops (*episkopountes*) in v.28. In 1 Peter 5:1,2 the presbyters are again, in most manuscripts, told to 'act as bishops' of the flock, though some important manuscripts omit the word *episkopountes*. If the word is not part of the original text its later inclusion is amazing, in view of the separation which was soon to come between bishop and presbyters. In 1 Timothy 3:1–7 we have a description of a bishop followed immediately by the requirements for a deacon, while in 1 Timothy 5:17–19 the former ministers are referred to and called presbyters. Titus, as we have seen, is told to 'appoint elders in every town . . . for a bishop must be blameless' (Titus 1:5–7). Jerome in his comment on this passage says bluntly *idem est ergo presbyter qui episcopus* – 'the bishop is therefore the same as the presbyter.' We can only draw the same conclusion from Philippians 1:1 with its 'bishops and deacons'. We can hardly imagine Paul singling out the first and third orders of ministry, omitting the second, and throwing in the extra anomaly of a plurality of bishops! Clement of Rome knows bishops and presbyters are identical. Like Paul in Philippians 1:1 Clement three times

mentions bishops and deacons together – and the whole
aim of his letter is to reinstate the deposed presbyters (Chs
42–44). In the *Didache* too, we meet just two orders,
bishops and deacons. As late as the fourth century
memories of this early usage survive. The *Apostolic Con-
stitutions* (2.26–8) maintain that it is the presbyters who
stand in the place of the apostles. This is not an anti-
episcopal claim; it is a recognition that in New Testament
times bishops and presbyters were identical.

The rise of the episcopate

How then did they get separated? Manifestly they very
soon did. Ignatius, whose lifetime certainly overlapped
considerably with that of St. John, shows that monepiscopacy, that is, rule by a single bishop, was a regular
feature in the churches of Asia Minor in his own day. As
bishop he relates to the bishops of Ephesus, Philadelphia
and so forth. He is almost obsessed with the importance of
the episcopate, and he often speaks with great clarity about
the threefold ministry. Thus in *Magnesians* 6 he pleads, 'Do
all things in unity, under the bishop presiding in the place of
God, the presbyters in the place of the council of the
apostles, and the deacons . . . who are entrusted with the
service of Jesus Christ.' He has nothing to say about
apostolic succession, though we learn from Tertullian
(*Adv. Marc.* 4.5) and Clement of Alexandria (in Eusebius
H.E. 3.23) that the apostle John went round in his old age
appointing bishops in Asia Minor. This seems very
possible. How else could bishops have become so marked a
feature in proconsular Asia within a decade of John's
death?

No doubt the very stridency of Ignatius's claims for
monepiscopacy indicates that it was not as firmly
established as he would like. It may well have come to the
West considerably later. The Roman church was, as we
have seen, governed by a board of presbyters in Clement's
day at the end of the first century, and the same held good
thirty or forty years later when Hermas wrote. He twice
refers to bishops, each time in the plural, and otherwise

speaks of the 'elders who preside over the church' (*Vis*. 3.5.1, *Sim*. 9.27.2, *Vis*. 2.4). It is significant that whereas Ignatius could write to the bishop in the Eastern churches, he could not do so at Rome. Nor could his contemporary, Polycarp. Although himself a bishop in the Ignatian sense (Ignatius, *Polyc*. 1.1) he knows that this form of church policy does not obtain at Phillippi. And so, with gracious Christian tact, he begins his letter, 'Polycarp and the presbyters with him, to the church of God sojourning at Philippi.' He makes no mention of the bishop anywhere in his letter, but refers to the Philippian leaders as 'presbyters' and 'deacons' (6.1,5.2). This was probably written in A.D. 115. It is plain that monepiscopacy was unevenly distributed in the first half of the second century. Thereafter it became universal.

The background of episcopacy

What is the background of this office that springs immediately to full flower in the pages of Ignatius? Nobody really knows. There is no obvious parallel in Judaism, though attempts have been made, unsuccessfully, to derive the Christian bishop from the *hazzan* of the synagogue or the *mebhakkér* of the Covenanters at Qumran. Several of the Fathers agree in seeing James of Jerusalem as the first bishop, or even as the 'bishop of bishops'. But James owed his position of undoubted supremacy at Jerusalem to his blood relationship with Jesus: this is underlined by the fact that when he was martyred in the early sixties 'Symeon, the son of Cleophas, our Lord's uncle, was appointed the second bishop, whom all proposed, as the cousin of the Lord' (Eusebius, *H.E.* 4.22). Clearly, we are dealing with a caliphate not an episcopate. James certainly furnished an obvious precedent for second-century bishops, with his central abode at Jerusalem, his wide supervision, and his constitutional rule along with the elders (Acts 21.18). Nevertheless by his physical connection with the Lord, and because of the destruction of his line in the early years of the second century, he actually represented the very antithesis of the emerging monepiscopacy of the Catholic Church.

If the precedents for the office are obscure, so are the stages by which it became separated from the presbyterate. However, if you have a board of elders, someone has to preside. Probably, therefore, the bishop soon emerged from the board of presbyters by virtue of his chairmanship. In the early days of the second century you find the bishop being associated with certain functions that would tend to emphasise his personal ascendancy. First, he is the man who presides at the Eucharist, where, from the nature of the case, you need a single celebrant. Second, he is always in charge of the property of the church. This consisted mainly in offerings at the Communion until the church began to own buildings at the end of the second century: it would be natural, therefore, for the celebrant to handle them. Third, we find the bishop acting as the focus of unity among the various sectional interests and the house-churches of a town. 'Do nothing without the bishop. Cherish Union; shun divisions,' pleads Ignatius (*Philad.7*). Fourth, he appears as the bastion of orthodoxy, the guardian of the apostolic faith; and this was particularly important before an authoritative canon of Scripture had emerged. The succession of bishops in a see was regarded, particularly by Irenaeus, as a safeguard against heresy and a guarantee of continuity with the teachings of the apostolic age. Finally, the bishop always appears as the foreign secretary, so to speak, of the church. Through him it communicates with others, and through him hospitality is afforded to visitors from other churches. In some such ways as these, we may believe, the chairman of the board of presbyters became the bishop of Catholic Christendom.

The purpose of episcopacy

But what was the theory that lay behind monepiscopacy? I believe that quite simply the idea of sole episcopacy originated in the sole oversight of God himself. In the New Testament *episkopē* and its cognates are referred to the Holy Trinity. It is exercised by Father, Son and Spirit

(Luke 19:44, 1 Pet. 2:12, 1 Pet. 2:25, Acts 20:28). *Episkopē*
is, therefore, an attribute of God. In his grace, he delegates
it without abdicating from it. Thus all Christians are called
to oversee or take care of one another (Matt. 25:36,43,
Jas. 1:27, Heb. 12:15). Like servanthood and priesthood, oversight belongs to the whole church. But the
church too, concentrates that care in the hands of its
ministers without its members abdicating from the responsibility of caring for others. The ministers representatively
take it on. No wonder Paul wrote 'If anyone aspire to
episkopē, he desires a noble task' (1 Tim. 3:1). No wonder
Ignatius exclaims that the bishop is the 'type', the representative of God, and rejoices with the Romans that after his
martyrdom the church in Syria will have God for its bishop
in his place! (*Magn.* 6.1, *Trall.* 3.1, *Rom.* 9.1). In short,
episkopē belongs supremely to God the Holy Trinity. He
shares it (without surrendering it) with the church, and with
its ministers in particular. The one bishop embodies in his
own person the oversight of God.

The value of episcopacy

Although therefore the Ignatian type of episcopacy cannot
be found in the New Testament nor in some parts of the
world for many years afterwards, nevertheless it remains
true that the New Testament knows and values the pastoral
oversight exercised by the apostles and their delegates over
local ministers. The need for this sort of oversight did not
diminish, but increased with the death of the last apostles.
We need a focus of unity within the churches of a given
area. We need an embodiment of the historic faith down
the ages and across the globe, and this is fittingly represented in a single person. We need someone who is
charged to defend the faith against attenuation or per-
version; though whether the episcopate has been very successful in this respect down the centuries may be doubted.
Most of all we need someone to care for the pastors of
hard-pressed local churches; and nobody knows this better
than the pastors themselves. On these grounds we can urge
that not merely the name but the office of bishop is

scriptural, primitive and of abiding value in the church.

In recent years this has become increasingly recognised among non-episcopal churches. There is value in monepiscopacy, and clearly it is the only form of church government that can possibly command universal assent in the reunion of Christendom. But that is not to say that episcopacy as traditionally exercised is ideal. The larger the diocese, the less justification there is for monepiscopacy. Sole leadership of a million or more people cannot possibly be pastoral, and runs great danger of becoming prelatical. Often counsel is darkened among advocates of episcopacy because the Ignatian arguments are applied to the present scheme of things in the West, and it is forgotten that episcopacy to Ignatius was more like a vicar's presidency over half a dozen curates than diocesan episcopacy where the bishop presides over hundreds of local churches. Ignatius does not speak to our condition, for he does not speak of our kind of bishops. If we wish to commend episcopacy we need to recover more of the sense of collegiality which Ignatius embodied. Twelve times in his letters he mentions the three orders of ministry; and in ten of them the three form an inseparable unity. Synodical government in England has gone some way towards regaining this unity, but there is still much too much decision-making in Diocesan Church House over matters which concern the parishes of the diocese, and the parishes themselves are not consulted. No wonder some Free Churchmen regard episcopacy with suspicion, even in this day and age. They feel, not without justification, that the undeniable tendency for the bishop to be transformed from an 'undershepherd' into the 'lord' of the flock is derogatory to the supreme headship of Christ over his church. The only type of episcopacy which can hope to win universal acclaim in the church of the future is one where the bishop is a leader who serves his people, shares decision making, and knows, loves and suffers with his flock.

Deacons

Our knowledge of deacons in the early church is as scanty

as it is of bishops, but for a different reason. As we have seen, service, *diakonia*, was the ideal and the task of every member of the church, and there was no immediate tendency to restrict the title to any particular group within it.

The word 'deacon' is used of Jesus himself (Rom. 15:8) and Paul uses it both of Timothy's ministry and of his own (1 Tim. 4:6,1:12). This should both remind us that all ministry in the New Testament is marked with the imprint of Jesus the Servant, and that the word is used of particular ministries only in a semi-technical sense.

An auxiliary ministry

Nevertheless, it is plain that the word was applied by the early Christians to subordinate ministries in the church: there are ministries of leadership and ministries of assistance. Deacons belong to the latter category. Leaving aside for a moment the question of whether the seven in Acts 6 were deacons in the technical sense, they are clearly an auxiliary and assistant ministry. The seven are set aside to *deacon* tables, thus releasing the apostles for their primary task of *deaconing* the word of God (Acts 6:4).

The same differentiation is to be found in 1 Cor. 12:28 in broad terms: while some are given by the Lord the task of being 'rulers' among his people, others are called to be 'helps'. To sharpen that distinction up a little, Paul speaks of 'bishops' and 'deacons' in Philippians 1:1 and 1 Timothy 3:8ff, though somewhat curiously in the very similar letter to Titus deacons are not mentioned.

The origin of the office is obscure. It seems to have been a Christian invention, otherwise Clement of Rome (ch. 42) would not have found it necessary to introduce deacons by force into the text of Isaiah 60:17! It would be nice to think that the seven of Acts 6 *were* the first deacons in the technical sense. For it would tell us that they were indeed a Christian invention; that they were ordained by prayer and the imposition of hands; that they had to be wise men full of the Holy Spirit; and that their functions beside being financial and administrative, involved preaching, apologetics and 'signs and wonders.' The later church certainly saw the seven as the first deacons, from Irenaeus onwards, so much so that the Council of Neo-Caesarea in A.D. 315 passed as one of its canons: 'The deacons ought to be seven, even if the city be great.'

Nevertheless it is a plain fact that the seven are not called 'deacons' in Acts 6; their functions of preaching and evangelism hardly correspond with the duties associated with the later diaconate; and when Philip, one of the seven, is mentioned later on in Acts he is called not 'the deacon' but 'the evangelist' (Acts 21:8). So we cannot be sure. But if the appointment of the seven is dissociated from the institution of the diaconate, we have no knowledge whatever of the origin of this office, and can only assume from Philippians 1:1 that this was the name given to a subsidiary office which assisted presbyter-bishops, particularly in financial matters. This would accord with their special mention in Philippians 1:1, for Philippians is a thank-you letter for a contribution given to Paul by the church at Philippi, of which the bishops and deacons were, no doubt, the organisers.

Their task

What were the functions of the deacons in the early Church? Whether or not the seven were deacons, the task of a subsidiary ministry engaged primarily in social work and poor relief accords well enough with such scanty references to their function as we find elsewhere in the New Testament. Deacons could be male or female: Romans 16:1 tells us Phoebe was a female deacon, while Pliny, a Roman governor writing a decade into the second century clearly refers to women deacons (*ministrae*). He tortured them in order to secure information about the Christians (Pliny, *Ep.* 10.96). 1 Timothy 3 says that a deacon must be consistent in what he says, serious about his Christian life, and not greedy for money: these were important qualities in a person who was constantly moving from house to house and distributing financial help. It was expected that deacons should be married and should manage their families

well. 'The women' also were to be serious about their
commitment, not greedy for money or wine, Christians
who had proved themselves and were reliable and not given
to gossip. It is not certain whether 'the women' means the
women deacons or the wives of the deacons – yet another
tantalising gap in our knowledge. We are not told that the
deacon must be talented at preaching or teaching, but we
are told that his life must be exemplary, his grasp on the
Christian faith comprehensive and his conscience tender.

In later generations we find the deacons closely associated with the bishop, whose assistants they became both
in liturgical and in administrative functions. This close
association with the bishop not infrequently led to a deacon
succeeding to the bishopric, occasionally without even
being ordained priest. Two things are never forgotten
about them: their embodiment of the ministry of Jesus the
Servant in his church, and their supposed origin in serving
tables. This was remembered both in the part they played in
administering the Holy Communion, and in the task which
Justin tells us fell to them afterwards, of taking the consecrated elements to any who were unable through sickness
to be present at the service (1 Apol. 65).

In the early church a man would often remain a deacon
for life, and so it is today in the Eastern Church where the
deacon does a 'lay' job. However, in the West the office
became a stepping-stone to the priesthood, as it still
remains in the Roman and Anglican Churches. At the
Reformation some attempt was made to recover the
primitive diaconate, and in Congregational and Baptist
Churches the 'deacon' denotes what the Presbyterian
Churches prefer to call 'elder'. This is a 'lay' office and does
not normally lead into the ordained ministry. Such a man is
the representative of the congregation who takes part with
the ordained minister in three ways in particular: assisting
in administering discipline, undertaking administrative
work, and distributing the elements at Holy Communion.
The diaconate is awaiting rediscovery in episcopal
churches, and it should become a serious subject for study
and research in denominations which profess such respect
for the threefold ministry.

Reform of the diaconate

Two possible ways ahead ought to be considered, as alternatives to the present system.

    If we have regard to the role of practical assistance which the deacons gave in the early church, we should perhaps allow the office to resume that character. Let men or women be made deacons not as a stepping-stone to the priesthood, but in recognition of the charism of practical assistance evidenced in their lives. Such a ministry might be paid or voluntary. An administrative assistant, a youth worker, a hostel warden in the ministry of a large church might well be paid. A churchwarden or treasurer if made deacon might not be paid. But in either case it would be the recognition by the church's leadership of the gifts bestowed upon a person for building up the Body of Christ through practical assistance. It would not be seen as stage one in the 'ordained' ministry of the church. This would remain in the hands of the presbyters.

    On the other hand, if we give more weight to the way in which the deacon was associated with the local bishop, especially in the administration of Communion, we might usefully reconstruct the diaconate in a different way. We have seen that the leadership of the local church was always plural in the early days, and that this is a healthy thing for any church. A group of experienced, reliable, local leaders in a congregation could be made deacons by the bishop, and, at his discretion and depending on need, be given licence to celebrate the Communion. This would provide a shared leadership team. It would give proper recognition to local church leaders who, unlike the vicar, will be living most of their lives in the area. It would enable a regular sacramental ministry to continue when the college-trained presbyter is likely to become increasingly rare in these days of inflation and financial stringency. These deacons would have no prerequisite or automatic intention of becoming full-time stipendiary clergy. They would remain local, theologically untrained assistants, but they could be of untold benefit in any congregation and could prevent many churches from closing or from being denied the sacraments. I foresee the day, not far away, when the college-trained man will be the co-ordinating factor between several such groups of experienced Christians who would undertake much of the leadership of the local churches.

If it be deemed too radical and too great a break with tradition to allow deacons to celebrate, even under the bishop's licence, then let such men be ordained 'priests', but remain in secular employment. The Anglican Church has already made some progress in this direction by allowing several ordination courses to take place locally with only the minimum of residential training, and by ordaining men to the Auxiliary Pastoral Ministry. This is encouraging, but the expedient is too new to be properly evaluated, and a good deal of development is needed. For one thing the wrong men seem to be chosen: they do not always come from the proven leadership of the local church but sometimes seem to be those who have an interest in church work and the time to pursue it. For another, their training leaves a lot to be desired: it represents a considerable additional load for a man who already has a busy professional life, and whose church responsibilities do not generally diminish. Some candidates in this training course almost become strangers to their families. Part of the trouble is that an attempt is made not to see what they really need for ministry, but to implant in them a potted version of what a young ordinand learns in three years at theological college. Moreover, predominantly intellectual, rather than pastoral, criteria still prevail in the minds of the selectors: how many of the apostles would have been recommended for training? And often when they are ordained such men are not properly used. There is frequently no sense of shared ministry with the vicar. There is often no consultation: they are merely asked to take services from time to time at the vicar's discretion. That is not a New Testament perspective of ministry.

Whichever expedient be adopted, there is a crying need for the diaconate to be rescued from oblivion and misuse. The church cannot afford to despise such concrete embodiment of the Servant ministry.

CHAPTER SIX

APOSTOLIC SUCCESSION?

The Ecumenical Movement is one of the most remarkable developments in the church of the twentieth century. Everywhere churches are looking towards reunion, though often taking several brisk paces backwards when it seems a possibility! There are, however three elements in the doctrine of the ministry which are proving serious barriers to reunion. Two are apostolic succession and sacrificial priesthood, and these two notions lie like submerged icebergs beneath the surface of all church unity discussions even if they are not manifestly brought into the open. The third is the matter of women priests. We shall examine these contentious issues in the next three chapters.

The place of apostles in the church

Before the resurrection

The word 'apostle' is so loosely used in current talk about 'apostolic orders' the 'apostolate of the laity' and so forth, that we need to glance at the place occupied by the apostles in the early church. That is not easy. We do not know how many there were; we know little of what they did after the early chapters of Acts; we do not know that the apostles had much to do with the administration of sacraments. They certainly baptised the first believers (Acts 2:41) but we know Paul was not in the habit of baptising (1 Cor. 1:14) and there is no evidence that they normally presided at the Eucharist, still less that a 'valid' Communion was impossible without the imposition of their hands upon the celebrant. Even the evidence that they made a habit of ordaining is less conclusive than we would like. Thus Telfer[1] finds in the New Testament 'no evidence that the presbyter-bishops could only become such by apostolic appointment, or that, when appointed, they received a laying on of apostolic hands,' and A. T. Hanson[2], in commenting on steps the apostles are supposed to have taken for preserving the ministry, asks: 'What steps did they take? Except for Paul, the only possible way in which the ministry could have been described as being perpetuated was in the presbyters of the Jerusalem church in Acts. But to describe these presbyters as successors of the apostles is absolutely fatal to the "Catholic" theory of the ministry. That is why everyone who tries to find evidence for the "Catholic" theory has to invent or discover a set of bishops (who were also called presbyters) to carry on the essential succession from the apostles to the bishops of the second century.'

One final problem is that the word 'apostle' seems to have been used for two different categories of people in New Testament days. The word means 'sent' and was conferred on special delegates sent out from a church (2 Cor. 8:23, Phil. 2:25, Acts 14:4,14, and often in the *Didache*). But it was of course used par excellence of the 'apostles of Jesus Christ', and it is with them that we are concerned.

The title is only very sparingly conferred on the twelve during the ministry of Jesus. They were primarily called that they might be with him, and only secondarily and subsequently sent forth by him to teach, heal and exorcise (Mark 3:14,15). They are represented throughout the ministry of Jesus as 'disciples', learners; they will be 'apostles' later, when their master is no longer with them. This happens in the Book of Acts when the title 'disciples' declines and that of 'apostles' becomes normal. The only exception to this reserve on the part of the Synoptists in calling the disciples 'apostles' during the ministry (John does not use the word at all) is the mission of the twelve, which is, so to speak, a dummy run for their apostolic ministry later on. They go forth clothed with Jesus' authority to do his work. Their message is his message, to proclaim the advent of the kingdom. Their role is his role, to be the Servant of the Lord and heal the sick, raise the dead, cleanse the lepers and cast out devils (Matt. 10:7,8, cf. 11:5 where Jesus's own role is precisely the same). During that mission of the twelve they are his representatives, clothed with his authority: 'he who receives you receives me' (Matt. 10:40). It is the shadow of things to come. But after that mission they become 'disciples' again, except that Luke solemnly points them out as apostles at the Last Supper when the new covenant is being inaugurated (Luke 22:14).

After the resurrection

After the resurrection the apostolic band take the place of Jesus (Matt. 28:18–20, Acts 1:8). They become witnesses to him just as he had been to the Father, and the Spirit bears witness along with them (John 15:26,27). They are led by that same Spirit into an understanding of the truth about Jesus, and so they become for the early Church the authoritative interpreters of the person and work of Jesus (John 14:26, 16:13–15). Thus the apostles become the norm of doctrine in the Church. 'That is why,' writes Cullmann[3], 'the New Testament attributes the same images to Jesus as to the apostles: *rocks* and the corresponding images of *foundations*, *pillars*. Never are these images used to designate the bishop.' So closely are they integrated with the person of their master that Cullmann can say 'the apostolate does not belong to the period of the church, but to that of the incarnation of Christ.' Indeed, so close is the identity between the Sender and the sent, that the New Testament can speak of the apostolic tradition as coming from the Lord himself. The exalted Lord proclaims through his apostles his own teaching and the extension of what he had said while on earth.[4]

In short, the apostles are historically unique and doctrinally normative for the church. Historically unique, because you cannot have more than one ground storey to a building. You cannot have more than one eyewitness generation. They afford the continuity between Christ and the church to balance the discontinuity of the ascension. Their place is unrepeatable. That is why they did not appoint other apostles in their place. It could not be done.

Not only historically unique: the apostles are doctrinally decisive for the church. The teaching of the church is the apostles' teaching, the fellowship of the church is the apostles' fellowship (Acts 2:42). They are the Lord's executors, his special delegates. They claimed this special position (see Gal. 1:6–12, 1 Thess. 2:13, 2 John 10, 1 Peter 1:11,12, Rev. 22:18ff), and this is what the subsequent church acknowledged when it canonised their writings. What is more, the subapostolic writers recognised this unique position which the apostles had. Clement of Rome says 'Christ is from God and the apostles from Christ' (1 *Clement* 42). Ignatius, his contemporary, writes 'I do not command you like Peter and Paul. They were apostles' (*Romans* 4). Bishop Serapion of Antioch wrote about A.D. 180, 'We accept the apostle as the Lord himself.' That attitude was typical of the early church. The apostles were decisive for the foundation and the beliefs of the church. What could not be shown to derive from apostolic circles was not to be imposed on any Christian as a necessary article of faith. We are bound to the apostles and their picture of Jesus. We cannot get behind it, even if we would. We believe because of their word (John 17:20). That is the historical succession to the apostles which Jesus envisaged. But in what other ways have the apostles successors?

Apostolic succession in the church

Four aspects of apostolic succession

There are several ways in which the question of succession to the apostles can be viewed. Looked at from one point of view, there are and can be no successors to the apostles. No other group of men shared the particularity of being with the historical Jesus on the one hand and witnesses to his resurrection on the other. Theirs was an unrepeatable 'bridge' function, and by definition it is unique. Moreover, the best understanding of the apostle against his background is that of the Jewish *shaliach*, the representative who comes with all the powers of his principal but who, when his commission is over, cannot further delegate but returns it to the sender. Accordingly there was no attempt made by the apostles to appoint other apostles in their stead.

Looked at from another point of view the apostles have a succession – in their doctrine. Their teaching was, as we have seen, decisive for the church. They were the privileged and inspired intepreters of Jesus, and we cannot pierce through to him except by means of their testimony. If we want to know what Christianity is and teaches, to the apostles we must go. The canon of the apostolic writings is the measuring rod of Christian truth. The apostles continue to rule the church through their writings. Men continue to believe because of their word (John 17:20).

Looked at from a third perspective there has been since the apostolic age a succession in the church of men who have been guardians of the apostolic deposit. Paul in the Pastoral Epistles was very anxious to see that Timothy conserved the apostolic teaching, and this was the earliest way in which a succession of bishops was justified. When Irenaeus began to value it at the end of the second century, it was not succession of hands imposed on the bishop which was at issue. It was the succession in office of bishops who safeguarded the teaching of the apostles against distortion and heresy from within the church and without. Bishops had, and continue to have, a primary task of defending the catholic faith of the apostolic church.

Looked at from a fourth perspective, there is a succession to the apostles in their supervisory role. The early church possessed, as we have seen, a settled local ministry of presbyters; it also possessed an itinerant ministry of oversight exercised primarily by the apostles themselves. We have also seen that at the end of the apostolic age, St John is reported to have gone round Asia Minor setting up bishops to carry on this circulating, supervisory role of the churches. And very important it is. The value of a 'pastor for the pastors' is too obvious to stress, and the majority of the world-wide church has made good use of it from that day to this. The bishop is to be valued as the symbol of continuity down the ages, and the focus of unity across the world church, of which he is a supervisory minister like the apostles. This aspect of the apostolic work is clearly capable of transmission: it has nothing unique and once-for-all about it.

A fifth, and controversial view

If in all these four cases there is succession from the apostles, why does the subject become so contentious in ecclesiastical discussions? Simply because there is yet another sense in which the phrase can be construed. This view claims that the apostles ordained bishops to succeed them, and that the historic episcopate, stretching back in unbroken succession to the apostles, is nothing short of essential to the church. Without such ordination it is impossible to exercise a 'valid' ministry or celebrate a 'valid' sacrament.

This view first came to the fore in Anglican circles with Newman's first *Tract for the Times* at the beginning of the Oxford Movement. The traditional exposition of the doctrine from then on has been that the threefold ministry is a divine institution stemming from the apostles and secured by an unbroken line of ordinations. The publication of *The Apostolic Ministry* in 1946, however, gave a new twist to the argument. It divided ministries into *essential* (i.e. those possessing unbroken links with the apostles) and all other ministries which were seen as *dependent*. Such a view was flattering to bishops, but damaging to the old 'Catholic' dogma of the threefold ministry.

Dix, the leading contributor to this important book, goes so far as to say that all the talk about the historic episcopate is beside the point. He recognises that Non-Conformist Churches should not be offered *episkopē*, for they have it already. He is not interested in the pros and cons of concentrating *episkopē* in the hands of a single individual; this he recognises to be unimportant, and potentially disastrous. 'What is really in question in our present discussions about episcopacy is not the episcopate at all. It is the apostolate,' he urges (p. 295). For Dix, together with Kirk in the introductory essay, argued that the essence of apostolic authority is its derivation from the Lord. The principle is plain; 'as the Father has sent me, so I send you.' The commission from Jesus was passed on by the apostles to the bishops, who are the custodians of it today.

Such, in essence, was the theory: it has been immensely influential. Dix unwisely bolstered it with the doctrine of the Jewish *shaliach*. He saw the apostle, rightly, against the background of this rabbinic official who came with plenipotentiary powers from his principal: thus 'he that is sent is as he who sent him.' Disastrous to Dix's position, however, was the fact that the *shaliach* could not transmit his authority. 'We are therefore forced to conclude,' writes Dr. Ehrhardt,[5] himself very sympathetic to Kirk's position, 'that unless Dr. Kirk abandons Rengstorf's[6] theory that the apostle was the *shaliach* of Christ, he cannot very well maintain the doctrine of apostolic succession.'

There is therefore some disarray in the internal arguments by which this exclusive claim for apostolic succession through the historic episcopate has been supported by Anglo-Catholics in recent years. It is probably true that only a small minority within Anglicanism understand, believe or care about the point. But the theory is constantly adduced by a very influential and vociferous minority, so it may be as well to ask it four questions. Is it biblical teaching? Is it sound theology? Is it historically demonstrable? Is it Anglican teaching?

1. *Is it biblical teaching*? Nobody has succeeded in demonstrating that apostolic succession in this exclusive sense is taught in the New Testament; and the Church of England, for one, does not require any man to believe as an article of faith what may not be shown from scripture (Article 6). It is true that Barnabas and Paul are once said to have appointed presbyters in every city they had evangelised on their first missionary journey. Very likely it was their regular practice, doubtless with the laying on of hands and

prayer. But we are never told the apostles had hands laid on them by Christ. We are never told that the ministry in all Christian communities had to wait for an apostle to come and authorise it. The New Testament indications, quite as much as the probabilities of the case, suggest that the first ministers in any congregation were appointed by the missionaries (often unknown folk, see Acts 8:1–4, 11:19–26) and then became self-recruiting. There was certainly a ministry at Rome and Antioch before these cities were visited by an apostle, and it is interesting to notice that when Paul left Philippi after his first visit, there was only a tiny group of new believers with no hint of any regular leaders (Acts 16); but when he came to write to the Philippians a few years later (without having visited them in between) there was a flourishing church complete with bishops and deacons. There is in the New Testament little ground for the view that apostolic authorisation was indispensable for ministry. To think in these terms is an anachronism. Not until the early third century did the doctrine of the manual transmission of the grace of orders begin to arise.[7]

Furthermore the holders of this view of apostolic succession consistently fail to recognise the diversity of practice in New Testament times. 'Primitive catholic uniformity' is nothing but a romantic myth. In point of fact, the prototype of 'catholic order' is represented by James and the Jewish church: the second-century episcopal lists mostly claim to go back to him. Paul, on the other hand, is interested in order but not in succession: he himself was in no succession. And a third discernible attitude to church order can be seen in the Johannine writings, where there are no special offices as such, and even the word 'apostle' has disappeared. The gift of the Spirit and the believers' love for the brethren replace them. There is no hint of succession in office as an indispensable element in Christian ministry.

Even if there were not this variety in the church order of the New Testament itself, the silence of scripture would be significant. If episcopacy were essential to the church, God would have made it clear to us.

2. *Is it sound theology*? The strength of this view of apostolic succession is that it takes the visible church of God, warts and all, with great seriousness. It is the society which Jesus left to carry out his work on earth. Nevertheless there are serious theological objections to the theory.

In the first place, it tends to limit the grace of God to episcopal communions, and is blind to the fact that God works just as significantly in non-episcopal churches. It simply will not do to dismiss this with talk of 'uncovenanted mercies' and the like.

Second, such a view is in grave danger of depersonalising the grace of God, and turning it into a substance which is transmitted through the correct pipeline. This is a serious declension from the New Testament concept of grace as God's personal and costly self-commitment to the undeserving.

Third, such a view leads to the conclusion that you can control the grace of God. You can organise it, domesticate it. If you think like this you run a serious risk of identifying external form with inner reality. Catholicism runs the same danger as Judaism, of supposing that the church stands by form and succession, not by inner reality and response to grace. Church authorities are always in danger of subordinating the spiritual and eschatological to the historical.

Fourth, the doctrine of apostolic succession reverses the New Testament picture of a ministry dependent upon the church. Instead we are presented with a church so dependent upon the ministry that if, in a period of massive opposition such as the Diocletian persecution, all Christian ministers had been rounded up and killed, that would have been the end of the church. Such a view borders on the ludicrous, but what else can Bishop Kirk mean when he writes, 'should such a ministry fail, the apostolic church, which is the Body of Christ in space and time, would disappear with it' (for the two are inextricably bound together)?[8] No, it is not merely the ordained ministry but the whole church which is heir to the command 'Go and make disciples of all nations.'

3. *Is it historically demonstrable*? Once again the

answer must be 'No'. Ignatius has a very high doctrine of
episcopacy but there is not a hint of apostolic succession in
his writings. The *Didache* (15.1) enjoins on congregations
the need to appoint *their own* bishops and deacons.
Clement of Rome knows that, at Corinth, the apostles
appointed a plurality of bishops or presbyters 'with a
further enactment that if they should fall asleep other
approved men should succeed to their ministry' (1 *Clement*
44.1,5). Irenaeus was consecrated not by another bishop
but by the council of presbyters in Lugdunum,[9] and this
practice of presbyteral consecration continued in
Alexandria as late as the fourth century.[10] The whole idea
of manual transmission of grace for orders is first found
among Latin Christian lawyers of the third century, men
like Cyprian, Tertullian, and later Augustine. Apostolic
succession was a legal fiction required by these legal minds
to connect the growing conceptions of the authority of the
clergy with the earlier days of Christianity. 'It served the
Christian lawyer in much the same way that another
curious legal fiction assisted the pagan civilian. The latter
insisted that the government of the Emperors from
Augustus to Diocletian was the prolongation of the old
Republican constitution; the former imagined that the rule
of bishops was the prolongation through the generations of
the inspired guidance of the original apostles who were
planters of the church.'[11] So much for a learned
Presbyterian summary of the situation: now for an
Anglican, no less learned. 'These Latin churchmen created
a historical myth, the unhistorical nature of which they
were secure from discovering. This was to the effect that
the apostles had provided for the future of the church by
creating an order of monarchical bishops. The first of these
they ordained, according to this myth, with their own
hands, and set them to govern the several churches with
which they were concerned.'[12]

4. *Is it Anglican doctrine*? In the first place it is important
to recall that the Church of England commits itself to
scripture as the source for necessary doctrine (Article 6).
This doctrine of apostolic succession cannot be derived

from scripture, so you would expect to find nothing in the
formularies of the Church of England to require its
acceptance. That is precisely what you do find.

Succession is not included in the marks of the Church
(Article 19). It is not mentioned in Article 23 which speaks
of ministering in the congregation. The Preface to the
Ordinal carefully refrains from unchurching non-episcopal
bodies, while giving good reason for the retention of a
threefold ministry in our own church. 'In these our doings',
says the Preface to the Prayer Book, 'we condemn no other
nations, nor prescribe anything but to our own people
only.'

The Reformers themselves freely intercommunicated
with their brethren in the Reformed and Lutheran
Churches on the continent. This practice continued for
more than 200 years. Bishop Joseph Hall, who in 1618
attended the Synod of Dort to represent the Church of
England, wrote in his book *Peacemaker*, 'There is no
difference in any essential matter between the Church of
England and her sisters of the Reformation. We accord in
every point of Christian doctrine, without the least
variation.' Richard Hooker, that most representative of
Anglican divines, prized episcopacy highly, yet refused to
conclude that it is absolutely necessary. 'The church hath
power by universal consent to take it (i.e. episcopacy)
away, if thereunto she be constrained through the proud,
tyrannical and unreformable dealings of her bishops', and
he is ready to recognise a ministry 'when God himself doth
raise up any, whose labour he useth without requiring that
men should authorise them.'[13]

This remained characteristic Anglican teaching, including most of the high church Caroline divines, until the
Oxford Movement.[14] In the first of his celebrated *Tracts for
the Times* Newman wrote of the bishop in ordination: 'he
but *transmits*; and thus the Christian ministry is a *succession*. And if we trace back the power of ordination from
hand to hand, of course we shall come to the Apostles at
last. We know we do, as a plain historical fact . . . We must
necessarily consider none to be *really* ordained unless they
have been *thus* ordained.'

The Anglo-Catholic doctrine of the exclusive validity of those orders which come from the apostolic succession was something quite novel within the Church of England. It is not doctrinally sound, scripturally based, historically reputable or part of the teaching of our Church. Indeed, the Anglo-Catholic historian Darwell Stone admits that it is impossible to argue 'that the present formularies and the post-Reformation English divines are committed to the necessity of episcopal ordination as distinct from the practical requirement in the Church of England.'[15]

The importance of the issue

It is important that these matters should be widely known in inter-church discussions. I have been engaged in many of these, and have been amazed by the way in which the Anglo-Catholic novelty of apostolic succession has been assumed by Non-Conformist Churches to be the teaching of the Church of England. It is no part of her teaching, and cannot be held to represent more than a minority view among some Anglicans. All Anglicans are committed to the value of episcopacy as a practical requirement in our Church. We are not committed to any theory about it, least of all to the view that it represents the continuation in our day of the authority of the apostles. For decades the Church of South India, though fully episcopal, was not granted intercommunion by the Church of England upon the insistence of Anglo-Catholics. It was second-class citizen in the episcopal club because some of its clergy had not been episcopally ordained. The future in reunion lies not with imparting episcopal ordination, reordination or conditional reordination to non-episcopal ministries, but the coming together, perhaps by solemn covenanting, of Churches whose members and ministers accept one another as Christ has accepted them. There is little doubt that episcopacy has a great deal to offer, as a symbol of unity and catholicity on the one hand, and as a pastoral office on the other. But it will not be accepted, nor should it be, if it comes with the implied or explicit rider that no other ministries are valid in the church of God.

While it is right to respect the views of minorities as far as possible, *is* it right to allow a view which was introduced into Anglicanism with the Tractarians, a view which led many of their most consistent thinkers to join the Church of Rome, to prejudice the reunion of the Anglican Church with her sister churches of the Reformation? And if it be argued that reunion with these churches on these terms would prejudice our eventual reunion with Rome and the Eastern Orthodox Church, this is an argument that must be resisted. For one thing these churches would prefer to negotiate with a united body rather than a series of disparate denominations. For another, they do not believe that Anglican orders are valid in the first place! They do not accept that we have the precious gift which we are so anxious to pass on to others. So reunion with other Reformation churches is unlikely to alter our future relations with Rome. There is great value in a bridge, provided it reaches both sides. But there is not much value in a 'bridge-church' as the Church of England delights to be, if it fails to reach either side. And that is precisely the danger the Church of England has been running since the Tractarian Movement alienated us from the Reformed Churches without gaining for us recognition from the 'Catholic' side.

CHAPTER SEVEN

SACRIFICING PRIESTHOOD?

As we saw in an earlier chapter, the word 'priest' is derived both in etymology and function from the 'elder' (*presbyteros*) of the New Testament. However, the word commonly has other associations; it means one who offers sacrifice. The Greek word for this person is quite distinct, *hiereus* (Latin *sacerdos*, from which we get sacerdotalism). This is not a matter of playing with words. It is a question of the meaning of Christian ministry.

Calvin complained of the Roman bishops that 'by their ordination they create not presbyters to rule and feed the people, but priests to offer sacrifice.' Roman Catholic theologians would not dispute this. The question is, does the Church of England do this? Is it official Anglican doctrine that the priest, duly ordained in the apostolic succession, has entrusted to him the authority and power to offer the sacrifice of the Eucharist? Because this conception of the priesthood in the Church of England is undoubtedly significant in any talks concerning unity with other Churches, we must examine both the testimony of the New Testament and the historic position of the Church of England on the matter.

Priesthood and sacrifice in the New Testament

The priesthood of Christ and his sacrifice

Jesus Christ sums up in himself all that was symbolised by the sacrificing priesthood of the Old Testament. He has himself so discharged the office of *hiereus* that no other priest will ever be needed. All agree on this matter nowadays, and that is solid gain. I suppose there is hardly a priest of any learning in the Anglican Communion these days who would argue the old mediaeval dogma of Catholicism that in the Eucharist the priest offers Christ for the sins of the living and the dead. It is now, thank God, universally recognised that Christ's priesthood is final and complete, and his sacrifice on the cross for man's salvation can neither be added to nor repeated. Thus A. G. Hebert, though arguing for a doctrine of eucharistic sacrifice, allows 'the sacrificial action is not any sort of reimmolation of Christ, not a sacrifice additional to his one sacrifice, but a participation of it,' and he repudiates the 'idea that in the eucharist we offer a sacrifice to propitiate God,'[1] So far so good. It is difficult to see how any other view could have gained ground in the light of the Epistle to the Hebrews, with its reiteration of the finality and sufficiency of Christ's sacrifice (Heb. 7:23–28, 9:24, 10:1–22). 'Christ thus abolishes all further human priesthood.'[2]

Indeed, any human priest would suffer from the same three defects which Hebrews finds in Jewish priests. He would in the first place be a sinner, needing forgiveness for himself and therefore unable to procure it for others (Heb. 7:26ff). Second, he could not offer a sacrifice acceptable to God, for that involves a perfect life, and there has ever only been one such (10:4–10 and 9:12, 10:12). And third, no man can maintain a satisfactory relation with God for others, because he dies. But Jesus can and does save those who come to God by him, because his eternal living presence guarantees their acceptance with God (Heb. 7:25). The priesthood of Jesus is thus unique, and his sacrifice unrepeatable.

The priesthood of all Christians and their sacrifice

I suppose that, given their grasp on the completeness of Christ's sacrifice and priesthood, it is not surprising to find the absence of any priestly caste within the early church. And yet, of course, it is simply amazing. These New

Testament writers were steeped in the sacrificial system of
the Old Testament, and yet never once do they use the
word *hiereus*, sacrificing priest, for any Christian minister.
The Aaronic model for Christian ministry lay obviously
close to hand. But they refused to use it. Just as the calling
of the Servant originally applied to all Israel, but shrank
and shrank until it was embodied in Jesus alone, and
thenceforward belonged distinctively to his Body, the
church; so it was with the priesthood. Originally all Israel
was called to be a nation of priests (Exod. 19:6) to bring the
world to God in prayer, and represent God to the world
through witness. But Israel did not fulfil her function;
neither did the Aaronic priesthood; neither did the high
priest himself. It was only Jesus who brought God to men
and brought back men to God.

But now his people share his role. They cannot, to be
sure, share his sin-bearing; that Christ fulfilled alone and
once for all. But in other ways the church can share. It
realises the ideal which eluded Israel, for the church is a
nation of priests (Rev. 1:6, 1 Pet. 2:9, cf. Exod. 19:6). What
that means is expressed in the New Testament in terms of
access, mediation and offering.

All Christians now enjoy unrestricted *access* to God.
In the Old Testament this had been the prerogative of the
high priest, once a year; with sacrificial blood he might
venture into the Holy of Holies. Now the way into that holy
place has been made available to all believers, through the
sacrifice of Christ (Rom. 5:2, Eph. 2:18, Heb. 4:16, 10:19,
1 Pet. 3:18). No other intermediary is needed.

All Christians also enjoy *the mediatorial role* of the
Old Testament priesthood. The priest represented God to
man and man to God. Very well, that role is now taken over
by the church, called to go into all the world and make
disciples on the one hand; and to intercede for all men on
the other (Matt. 28:19, 1 Tim. 2:1). This two-way
mediation of evangelism and prayer is the solemn lifelong
calling of the church, which is a 'royal priesthood, a holy
nation, God's own people' (1 Pet. 2:9). It is significant that
these two activities are both spoken of as priestly ministries
in the New Testament (Rom. 15:16, Rev. 8:3ff).

In the third place, the church, and every Christian in it, inherits *the priestly task of offering* gifts and sacrifices to God (1 Pet. 2:5). Of course, this had always been the task of the priest under the Old Covenant (Heb. 8:3). The sacrifices of the church which the New Testament mentions are praise and thanksgiving, faith, almsgiving, a godly, generous life, evangelism and supremely the sacrifice of ourselves (Heb. 13:5, Phil. 2:17, Acts 24:17, Heb. 13:16, Rom. 15:16, 12:1,2).

Two points are to be noted about this priestly work of the church. In the first place it belongs to every Christian, not to any ministerial group. Secondly, 'Our offerings are not propitiations, for nothing that we could do could have turned away God's wrath. It is solely because of what God has done that we are able to approach him and bring offerings in which he will take pleasure. It is because of Christ's one, true, effective sacrifice offered once for all, that our unworthy oblation is possible.'[3]

The priesthood of ministers and their sacrifice

Priesthood is never associated with *presbyters* in the New Testament. Christian ministers are no more and no less priests than any other members of Christ's priestly Body. The idea of a priestly ministerial caste came into Christianity from pagan sources,[4] and was furthered by sacrificial analogies from the Old Testament. It was not until Cyprian in the middle of the third century that we find the word *hiereus* being regularly used of the Christian minister.

Furthermore, the Eucharist is never in the New Testament called a sacrifice, though of course the death of Christ, which it displays, was *the* sacrifice for sins. But the Holy Communion is not seen as one of the many things we offer to God. It is primarily something he offers to us. That is why it is called a sacrament of the *gospel*. The prime movement both in the gospel and this, its sacrament, is from God to man, and not from man to God – a form of Pelagianism which has considerable currency these days. Take, for example this irenic but still misleading statement by Dr. Hebert, quoted with approval by the Lambeth

Bishops of 1958: 'The true celebrant is Christ the high priest, and the Christian people are assembled as members of his Body to present before God his sacrifice, and to be themselves offered up in sacrifice through their union with him.' The bishops go on to say, 'We are partakers of the sacrifice of Christ. Christ with us offers us in himself to God.' Let us examine such claims.

First, when it is suggested that the church offers to God Christ's unique offering, this is a concept quite alien to the New Testament, which sees Christ as the one who made that sacrifice not *with* us but *for* us when he took the world's sin upon himself at Calvary and then sat down in the place of honour and victory at the Father's right hand. We must not suppose, in order to evade this point, that Christ continues to offer his sacrifice on the heavenly altar as the church offers it on the earthly altar; this view of Moberley, Hicks and Bicknell has not one whit of scriptural support. According to the imagery of Hebrews there is no altar in heaven any more than there was in the Holy of Holies (Heb. 9:24). Jesus is not constantly offering to the Father his sacrifice once made. Chrysostom rightly says, 'Do not think because you have heard Jesus is a priest, that he is always offering sacrifice. He offered sacrifice once and for all and thenceforward he sat down.'[5] But does not the New Testament say that Jesus is praying for his people? Indeed it does, in two important places, Romans 8:34 and Hebrews 7:25. But in each of them the same rare and significant word is used, *entunchanō*. It means that Christ *is around* on our behalf, not that he is asking for our acceptance as from a Father reluctant to grant it.[6] His *presence* is his plea for us. Westcott saw long ago what it did and did not mean. 'The modern conception of Christ pleading in heaven his passion, offering his blood on behalf of men, has no foundation in Hebrews. His glorified humanity is the eternal pledge of the absolute efficacy of his accomplished work. He pleads by his very presence on the Father's throne.'[7]

Our problems here are partly linguistic. Christ does not *plead* his sacrifice in the normal sense of the word because it is already accepted and attested by the resurrection.

But he can properly be said to plead it if by that is meant that his presence as the Lamb once slain in the midst of the throne is the silent plea for our acceptance. He does not *present* his sacrifice, if by that is meant that he continues to offer to the Father his sacrifice on Calvary. But he may rightly be said to present it, and so may we, if that is meant to draw attention to and celebrate the sacrifice once offered.

A second ambiguous phrase is the talk of 'uniting our sufferings' or 'joining our offerings' with those of Christ. This can so easily detract from the uniqueness of Christ's work. His sufferings were atoning, ours are not. His sacrifice removed the sin of the world, ours does not. The New Testament wisely does not speak of our 'offering Christ' or 'presenting his sacrifice'. We do not, in the eyes of the New Testament, associate ourselves and our offering of fitful obedience with his perfect sinlessness which removed the world's sin. We are indeed 'partakers of Christ's sacrifice' but partakers only in the *benefits* that flow from it, not in the *making* of it. Our self-offering is not part of Christ's self-offering, but a grateful response to his prior act.

This leads us on to an important distinction which must be emphasised if we talk at all about eucharistic sacrifice. Such language comes to us from the Old Testament. The Old Testament knew two different types of sacrifice. There was the sin offering which turned aside God's wrath, and the burnt offerings and meal offerings which were a sweet-smelling savour to God. The sacrifice of Christ fulfilled both types of Old Testament offering. Viewed as a sin offering, his sacrifice was complete and unrepeatable. Viewed as a burnt offering, it was unique in its perfection, but not in its character, for it was the pattern and the ideal of our own self-offering (Eph. 5:2). In this latter sense we do share with Christ in self-oblation. It is because Christ's sacrifice was at the same time expiatory and dedicatory, whereas ours is only the latter, that confusion arises. His atoning sacrifice is the *root* of our salvation. Our responsive sacrifice of praise, thanksgiving and surrender are the *fruit* of it. The two must never be confused.

It is true that in the second and third centuries Christians often spoke of the Holy Communion, as well as prayer, evangelism and so forth, in sacrificial terms. But they did not suggest that our sacrifice is incorporated in Christ's. Instead they saw the Eucharist as the fulfilment of Malachi 1:11 and the Old Testament meal offering. It was a 'sacrifice of thanksgiving' which the church 'offers to God for having made the world and all that is in it for man's sake, and also for having set us free from evil.'[8] And the Fathers take up the image of the Old Testament meal-offering which was given by the leper once he was cleansed from his disease; this is the thanksgiving sacrifice they see in the Eucharist.

In short, the Christian priesthood is, in F. D. Maurice's distinction (taken over by J. B. Lightfoot) 'representative without being vicarial'. That is to say, when a presbyter celebrates the Communion he is exercising the double representative function which, as we saw, characterises the priesthood of all believers. He acts on behalf of the Lord when proclaiming pardon and performing the actions with which Christ instituted the sacrament. He acts on behalf of men when he leads the prayers and praises and presents the offerings of the congregation. He is acting as a representative. He does not thereby take away the layman's right of direct access to God, nor of assuring a penitent of God's pardon. When the minister acts as God's mouthpiece 'he does not interpose between God and man in such a way that direct communication with God is superseded on the one hand, or that his own mediation becomes indispensable on the other.' And when he acts as the mouthpiece of the congregation, as 'the delegate of the priestly race . . . here too his function cannot be absolute and indispensable. It may be a general rule . . . that the highest acts of congregational worship shall be performed through the principal officers of the congregation. But an emergency may arise when . . . the layman will assume functions which are otherwise restricted to the ordained ministry.' Such is Bishop Lightfoot's conclusion.[9] I do not believe that any other is consonant with scripture.

Priesthood and sacrifice in Anglican teaching

Cranmer, the architect of the Prayer Book, has this to say of Christian priesthood: 'The difference between the priest and the layman in this matter is only in ministration; that the priest, as a common minister of the church, doth minister and distribute the Lord's Supper unto other, and other receive it at his hand.'[10] Logically, therefore, he used the words 'priest' and 'minister' interchangeably in the Prayer Book. This has been done in the modern services of the Alternative Service Books, current in most parts of the Anglican Communion, and the use of 'presbyter', 'celebrant' and 'president' as synonyms for 'priest' go a long way to help those coming from backgrounds which are not Anglican.

Of sacrifice Cranmer has this to say:

One kind of sacrifice there is which is called a pro-pitiatory or merciful sacrifice, that is to say, such a sacrifice as pacifieth God's wrath and indignation, and obtaineth mercy and forgiveness for all our sins . . . And although in the Old Testament there were certain sacrifices called by that name, yet in very deed there is but one such sacrifice whereby our sins be pardoned . . . which is the death of God's Son, our Lord Jesus Christ; nor ever was any other sacrifice propitiatory at any time, nor never shall be. This is the honour of this our priest wherein he admitted neither partner nor successor.

Another kind of sacrifice there is, which doth not reconcile us to God, but is made of them that be recon-ciled by Christ . . . to show ourselves thankful to him; and therefore they be called sacrifices of laud, praise and thanksgiving. The first kind of sacrifice Christ offered to God for us; the second kind we ourselves offer to God by Christ.[11]

With that clear distinction in mind Cranmer con-structed the Communion Service. No mention of the sacrifice of 'ourselves, our souls and bodies' was made until after reception of the elements which display 'his one full, perfect and sufficient sacrifice, oblation and satisfaction for the sins of the whole world.' Our sacrifice is clearly responsive, made possible by his own.

If this was the view of Cranmer, what of the judicious Hooker? 'I rather term the one sort (of clergy) *presbyters* than *priests*, because in a matter of so small moment I would not offend their ears to whom the name of priesthood is odious, though without cause.' Hooker then explains the derivation of priest from *presbyteros* but admits that it has often been associated with sacrifice. He continues:

> Seeing then that sacrifice is now no part of the church ministry, how should the name of priesthood be thereunto applied? Wherefore whether we call it a priesthood, a presbytership, or a ministry, it skilleth not: although in truth the word *presbyter* doth seem more fit, and in propriety of speech more agreeable than *priest* with the drift of the whole gospel of Jesus Christ.[12]

It would be tedious to show how this view remained characteristic of the Church of England until the Oxford Movement. This has been superbly done by Professor Norman Sykes in *Old Priest and New Presbyter*. It cannot be denied that at the Reformation the notion of a sacrificing priesthood within the church was firmly repudiated. Indeed at the ordination of a priest, the mediaeval habit of presenting the man with a chalice and patten was significantly changed. From now on he was given a Bible. It is hardly surprising therefore that Anglican orders are condemned by Rome because they lack the intention to make a man a priest in the sacrificial sense. The old priest has become the new presbyter. That is the position of the Church of England. Whatever the views of some of her members, a Church's doctrine must be judged by her formularies. There is no doubt that the formularies of the Church of England (the Bible, the Book of Common Prayer, and the Articles of Religion), do not favour the interpretation of priesthood and sacrifice advocated by 'Catholic' Christendom. Newman began the Oxford

Movement convinced that he could, by subtle casuistry, reconcile the Articles with the Council of Trent. He later realised the dishonesty of such an attempt, and left the Anglican for the Roman fold.

The Anglican Church has a wonderful and proper comprehensiveness. It is important to show that those with quite widely different viewpoints can live and work together within a single communion, thus demonstrating that Christian love and fellowship go deeper than theological differences. But those Anglicans who do not adopt Tractarian views of the ministry and sacraments have a right to ask that comparatively recent intrusions into the historic ethos of Anglicanism should not be regarded as the quasi-official view of the Church. Neither apostolic succession nor eucharistic sacrifice will stand close investigation in the light of scripture and Anglican tradition, and they ought not to be allowed to stand in the way of an unequivocal recognition of those ministries of orthodox Christian communions which do not claim to stand within the historic succession or to be offering sacrifice in their Eucharists.

CHAPTER EIGHT

WOMEN IN MINISTRY?

In many countries these days the question of women in Christian ministry has become an explosive issue. This is a reflection of the social turmoil over women's liberation, and whereas liberal opinion in the churches tends to follow the liberation attitudes of society in general, conservative opinion tends to take the position that the Bible is against women's ministry. This is a confused and contentious area: but it will not go away. It is important therefore to concentrate our attention on the biblical material and see how far it affirms and how far it confronts prevailing social attitudes.

The background

Women were not highly prized in either Hebrew or Graeco-Roman society. In the latter, women were under the authority of either their father or their husband; their education was slender; they could not testify in a court of law; they could not inherit property. In the Hebrew world, it was not much different. Women had no rights, no education. They were segregated in the synagogue and could not hold office in it. If anything their position deteriorated as the centuries went on, and the rabbis taught that it was better to burn the Law than to teach it to a woman, while men thanked God daily that they were not created a heathen, a slave, or a woman.

However, by the first century A.D., the old religion of Rome was in decay and was being replaced with a multitude of cults from the east, some of them orgiastic and most of them giving an unhealthy prominence to women. Scandals were not infrequent and Roman society looked on them with fascination but suspicion. The teaching we have in the New Testament on women in ministry (and there is not a great deal of it) was largely directed by Paul to ladies in Ephesus (the Pastoral Epistles) or Corinth (the Corinthian correspondence). Both places had particular and unsavoury reputations. The goddess Diana was, in Ephesus, far from the chaste huntress of Greek folklore; she was the many-breasted fertility cult figure, worshipped with sensuality in order to gain union with the life principle and ensure fertility for the crops. Corinth was a sailors' port as well as being an Oriental city and a Roman capital. It was dominated by a hill, the Acrocorinth, where Venus was worshipped as prostitute by a thousand courtesans. It is hardly surprising that against such backgrounds the New Testament writers were not enthusiastic about encouraging feminism.

The Jesus revolution

Xenophon in the *Oeconomicus* (7ff) shows us what the lot of the normal woman was like: it did not change much in the centuries that followed. Isomachus is explaining to Socrates why his bride, aged fifteen, needs instruction in running the house. 'She had spent the previous part of her life under the strictest restraint, in order that she might see as little, hear as little and ask as few questions as possible.'

The contrast with the Gospels could not be greater. Jesus revolutionised the status of women by the way he acted towards them. The portraits of Mary his mother, and Elizabeth, mother of John the Baptist, are most sensitively drawn. In St. Luke's Gospel, particularly, we are confronted by women at every turn. Anna the prophetess (Luke 2:36–8), the widow of Nain (7:11–17), the marvellous story of the woman in Simon's house who washed Jesus's feet with her tears (7:36–50), and Mary Magdalene, from whom Jesus expelled seven demons (8:2). We are introduced, albeit briefly, to society ladies from court, including Joanna and Susanna who followed Jesus around and provided for him and his followers, sometimes at least, from their substance (8:3). Jesus bothered about the woman with the issue of blood and the dying girl (8:41–48). He noticed the widow with her two mites and commended her giving above all the public benefactors of the day (21:1–4). We find him relaxing in the home of close friends, Mary, Martha and Lazarus (10:38–42) and these figure more largely in St. John's Gospel. When the 'daughters of Jerusalem' wailed at his impending execution he showed more compassion for them than for himself (23:27–31), and at his death it was the women who remained round the cross, supporting him with love while the men ran away (23:49). The women observed how his body was laid in the tomb, and went away to prepare spices to bring with them on what proved to be Easter morning (23:55).

The attitude of Jesus to women was staggering. He did not treat them like chattels, but like equals. When asked his thoughts on contemporary divorce, so totally weighted in favour of the man, he repudiated it entirely, taking his hearers back to the 'one-man one-woman for ever' concept of Genesis 2:24. The *imago dei* lay in the harmonious interrelationship of man and woman in God's creation, not in domination of one by the other.

Women were the first witnesses of the resurrection (Luke 24:1ff), and were the first to be entrusted with proclaiming it (Matt. 28:1). Jesus revealed himself first to Mary in the garden outside the tomb (John 20:1ff). We find the women next at prayer with the apostles (Acts 1:14). They were waiting for the outpouring of God's Spirit on sons and daughters alike (2:17) and they were not disappointed, for they too received the power, the gifts and the indwelling of the Spirit on the Day of Pentecost (2:1ff). We find them owning houses which they use as Christian worship centres (12:12). We find them, along with their husbands, selling property (5:1). Paul's first convert in Europe was a distinguished businesswoman, Lydia (16:14). Priscilla, who often in the New Testament is mentioned

before her husband Aquila, joined him in instructing
Apollos in the faith, and their homes in Rome, Corinth and
Ephesus were centres of Christian worship and teaching.
We find women like Mary, Tryphaena and Tryphosa en-
gaging in active propagation of the Christian cause,
'labouring in the Lord' (Rom. 16:6, 12). We find them
associating with Paul in spreading the gospel (Phil. 4:3,
Acts 18:1ff), and it is hard to imagine this did not sometimes include preaching. We find them assisting in the
leadership of the church by means of the two defined roles
of deacon and widow (1 Tim. 5:3ff., 9–17; 3:8–13; Rom.
16:1; Pliny *Ep*. 10.96). It is clear from 1 Timothy 5:9 that
the widows were to be enrolled for service as well as being
supported financially. The Greek New Testament does
not, moreover, coin a female derivative of 'deacon' for the
woman holder of that office, as we do with 'deaconess'. She
is simply 'deacon' irrespective of gender (Rom. 16:1). And
Phoebe, referred to there, was clearly a woman of substance and influence, since she is called *patrona* (the senior
partner in the famous patron-client relationship in Roman
society). This would have involved her in a leading role in
society and as deacon she also shared in the leadership of
the church. 'She has been a helper of many, and myself as
well' says Paul in commendation of this lady, as she goes to
Rome as the representative of the Corinthian church.
Clearly, it will not do to suppose women had no role in the
church of the first century.

But we can go further. Women both pray in church
(which they could never have been allowed to do in
Judaism) and utter prophetic messages (1 Cor. 11:5). The
four daughters of Philip the evangelist all had the prophetic
gift, and their fame spread far and wide (Acts 21:9). To be
sure, there were dangers here. The church at Thyatira was
plagued by a woman with prophetic pretensions who led
people astray: she was like the Old Testament Jezebel
(Rev. 2:20). This sort of person was a great embarrassment
to the Christian cause, which may help to explain Paul's
caution about women in ministry, not least in Ephesus and
Corinth. In Philippi and Rome the problems appear to
have been less.

The position of women

The position of women is abundantly clear in the New Testament. They are 'joint heirs of the grace of life' (1 Pet. 3:7). The clearest manifesto of the position of women is given by that supposed misogynist, St. Paul. 'There is neither Jew nor Greek, there is neither slave nor free, there is neither male nor female; for you are all one in Christ Jesus' (Gal. 3:28). This totally upsets the Jewish assumption of male superiority, in which, by the way, Paul himself had been reared. Man and woman are completely equal before God. But he means more than this. That equality has to have practical outworking, just as it does in the other two antitheses. If all are indeed one in Christ, the agelong prejudices must be abolished. Galatians 3:28 is the fundamental presupposition against which all Paul's other teaching about women must be seen.

There are three highly paradoxical elements in Paul's teaching about women over the range of his letters. First, equality versus subordination in marriage. Second, silence in church contrasted with ministry in church. Third, some teaching role or none. Let us look at these one by one.

Subordination?

First the question of subordination. Paul has a lovely understanding of the marriage relationship as one of total complementarity: 'In the Lord, woman is not independent of man, nor man of woman; for as woman was made from man, so man is now born of woman' (1 Cor. 11:11). Both owe their existence to the other and cannot do without the other. Male and female chauvinism is excluded, so is 'unisex': complementarity and partnership are the purpose of God for the sexes. But how can that be reconciled with Paul's teaching on the woman's subordination in marriage? In 1 Corinthians 11:3 Paul speaks of three headships: the same relationship subsists between wife and husband, between mankind (or perhaps 'the husband') and Christ, between Christ and the Father. In all three there is equality of life and subordination or differentiation of function. Christ is the 'head' over man: the husband is 'head' over his

wife. There is nothing derogatory about this. It is paralleled
by the Father's 'headship' over Jesus. In each of these three
relationships we see shared life and different roles.

In Ephesians 5.21ff Paul takes it further. To our
amazement he expounds the whole relationship of man and
wife in terms of 'subjection'. But there is no trace of
chauvinist triumphalism. *Both are to be subject to one
another!* That is what verse 21 says: 'be subject to one
another out of reverence for Christ.' In other words, the
wife is to treat the husband as she would treat her Lord.
And the husband is to treat his wife as Jesus would. And
then Paul begins to spell out what this mutual subjection
will mean. For the wife it will involve three things. She will
defer to her husband as she would to the Lord (Eph.
5:22,24). She will *cleave* to him as she would to the Lord
(v.31). She will *respect* him as she would the Lord (v.33).
But if this is to be the proper attitude in the wife, the
husband must merit it, as Christ does. He too must
subordinate his own desires for the sake of his wife. The
form his submission takes is different but just as costly. He
must *protect* his wife, as Christ protects or 'saves' his spouse
the church (v.23). He must *sacrifice* himself for her, as
Christ did for us (v.25). And he must *cherish* her as his own
body: that is what Christ does for his Body and bride the
church (v.29). It is only to such loving self-sacrifice that the
wife is told to submit. It is only self-giving love which
deserves anything of the sort.

It should be clear that Paul has the highest view of
marriage and the deepest respect for women. The wife is to
the husband what the church is to Christ. It is impossible to
go higher than that. Equally he is clear that in the family
(and he is not talking about men and women as such but
about husband and wife within the marriage bond) it was
the task of the man, not the woman, to lead (1 Cor. 11:3;
Eph. 5:22). Try it the other way round and ask yourself if he
was wrong!

Silence?

Second, what about the contradictory instructions to

women in church? On the one hand he allows women to
pray and prophesy in church (1 Cor. 11:5). On the other he
tells them to keep silent in church (1 Cor. 14:34). Or does
he? Notice that in 14:34 he is speaking to wives, not women
in general; the context makes this perfectly plain ('let them
ask their husbands at home') although the same Greek
word does duty for 'woman' and 'wife'. Is he contradicting
himself flatly within three chapters? I think not.

Consider the background. Christian families from a
Jewish background and proselytes too (the richest field for
evangelism in the first century) would always have been
separated in synagogue: the women would have been put in
the gallery. Remember, too, that the woman had no
education to speak of. All this gradually changes as the
Christian movement begins to find itself. Men and women
mix in the assembly for worship. And the women, who had
been kept down for so long, now begin to assert themselves, particularly in asking questions. This brings disorder and delay in the worship. So Paul bids them keep
silent with their chatter in church and ask their husbands at
home. This is perfectly compatible with allowing and
encouraging female participation in and even leading of the
worship.

Teaching?

Third, how about the apparent ban on women teaching in
mixed audiences, according to 1 Tim. 2:12? 'I permit no
woman to teach or to have authority over men; she is to
keep silent.' How can that be reconciled with what was
happening in Paul's own assemblies and with Paul's own
approval? The answer lies, I think, in the meaning of the
word *authentein*, normally translated 'have authority over'.
It is clearly a key word in this passage, and the passage is
crucial to the supposedly scriptural argument that a woman
must not by teaching 'exercise authority' over men. The
word occurs only here in the New Testament. What does it
mean?

The background of the word is one of sex and murder,
not authority at all! In Greek writers like Euripides,

Philodemus and Phrynicus the word is frankly erotic; the
same is true of Wisdom 12.6. John Chrysostom in his
commentary on the passage in 1 Timothy 2 understood it in
these terms. If Paul is not allowing women in orgiastic
Ephesus to slaughter men by leading them into cultic for-
nication through their teachings, that is a very different
matter from a blanket teaching prohibition. And that
seems to be the case. The Thyatiran 'Jezebel' taught people
to fornicate and led them into spiritual slaughter (Rev.
2:20ff). The Book of Proverbs had been very clear that the
prostitute's house was the highroad to slaughter (Prov.
2:18, 5:5, 7:27), and murder is one of the other well-
attested meanings of *authentein*. In this rare word the
murderous and the erotic combine. This interpretation
makes sense of the whole context in 1 Timothy 2. Women
are told to dress modestly in a city where there were many
courtesans (vv.9, 10). They must learn to live in a Christian
way in subjection to the gospel ('silence'). They must
realise that there is only one way to have union with God,
through Jesus Christ (v.6) not through the cult prostitution
they had once practised. (Incidentally, the Fathers used
this rare word *authentein* to describe such cult prostitution[1].)
They must practise their faith in quiet decorum, not with
the orgies demanded by Ephesian religion. The devil had
'seduced' Eve (the verb used in v.13, 14 very frequently has
sexual overtones): let them take care. Verse 15 might refer
to the social and economic rescue or 'salvation' of these
women through marriage and the family, or perhaps to
concern for the illegitimate children brought into the world
through their liaisons. In the Book of Wisdom reference
authentein refers to 'parents engendering helpless souls'.
Maybe Paul knew and caught the allusions of that Wisdom
passage; maybe he was moved to reflect that the gospel of
the Saviour could rescue not only the mother from the grip
of immorality but the child from the stigma of illegitimacy.
Both personalities could be healed by the gospel; and faith,
love, holiness and self-control would grow in those who
once were women of the streets.

It is not possible to demonstrate that this is the correct
interpretation of this difficult passage. But it makes sense.

It does justice to the Greek, to the thought of Paul, to the power of the gospel, and to the meretricious background of places like Corinth and Ephesus. Moreover it removes a glaring inconsistency from an apostle who clearly did use women in ministry, and yet in this passage appears to deny them any part in it. If it is even a serious possibility, it should loosen up a great many restrictive attitudes among Christians who genuinely want to be guided by scripture in this matter. At least it will make us think again, and perhaps ensure that Christianity which was in the van of women's liberation in the first century does not remain one of the last bodies in the world of the twentieth century to allow women a significant place in leadership.

Women in ministry

Women's ministry in the New Testament

We have seen that the gospel of Jesus revolutionised the place of women. Naturally something like that would take some time to work through, particularly against backgrounds of deep prejudice. But even so, it is remarkable to see how far and how fast the early Christians moved.

Women engaged in the ministry of prayer, not only privately but publicly in the congregation (1 Cor. 11:5). That was a remarkable departure from precedent.

Women engaged in the ministry of prophecy. This had been dead for centuries, but revived at the birth of Jesus, and the New Testament is full of this direct communication by God with his people through the words of one member. Women as well as men took part in this and thus were honoured, in the prophetic role, as second only to apostles (1 Cor. 11:5, 12:28, Acts 21:9).

Women engaged in the ministry of teaching. Sometimes men have argued that women are constitutionally unable to teach Christian doctrine with balance and insight: they conclude that this accounts for Paul's prohibition in 1 Timothy. Nothing could be further from the truth. The

Pastoral Epistles themselves show widows 'teaching what is good' (to whom is not specified) as well as 'training younger women' (Titus 2:3–5). Their role in teaching within the family is shown by 2 Timothy 1:5; 3:14.

Women engaged in the ministry of personal counselling. Priscilla and Aquila used their home to help Apollos to Christian maturity (Acts 18:26).

Women engaged in the ministry of hospitality. A good example of this is John Mark's mother and the way in which her home became a centre for Christian work in Jerusalem (Acts 12:12).

Women engaged in acts of charity: a lady like Dorcas gained a tremendous reputation for this. She seems to have made clothes to give away, in addition to other good works (Acts 9:36–41). A number of women are mentioned in Romans 16 as having laboured much in the Lord: this social involvement may have been one of the ways in which they exercised their ministry.

But they were also effective in evangelism. This is noticeable in northern Greece where women had more freedom in any case. Lydia, Euodia and Syntyche were three remarkable women in the Philippian church, and the latter two, Paul says, 'wrestled with him in the gospel' (Phil. 4:3) which must mean strenuous evangelistic endeavour.

On top of all this women could be deacons, as we have seen. Phoebe held this office in the church at Cenchreae (adjoining Corinth), and appears to have been Paul's delegate in taking the Letter to the Romans to the church in the capital. The context of 1 Timothy 3:11 and the way it is phrased makes it likely that Paul is speaking not of the wives of deacons (to whom he alludes in v.12) but to women deacons. Certainly this is how the Greek Fathers understood the verse, and we know from Pliny's letter (*Ep*. 10.96) that there was such an order in the church. Their value was immense especially in an oriental culture which required a high degree of segregation between men and women. In later times they visited, instructed and assisted at the baptism of women candidates. No doubt their role in the early days was not dissimilar.

Women's ministry now

If, then, women could lead the prayers, evangelise, prophesy, engage in social relief, teach and hold the office of a deacon in the early church, what should we make of the current move towards their ordination?

There is one obvious preliminary point to make. That is, for all their full involvement in the ministry of the early Christians, and for all their manifest equality with men in Christ, we do not find them occupying the front line in leadership. There are no women apostles, no women presbyters: there are women deacons and helpers of various sorts. Theirs was a ministry of support.

However, granted that in those days it would have been going too far too fast to ordain women, what about the present situation? How should we apply New Testament material to the present crisis about ordination? Should the fact that women were not presbyters weigh more with us than the fact that their position was clearly revolutionised by the gospel?

A new look to ordination

I believe we find it hard to answer the question about female ordination not just because of the ambiguous biblical material, the confused social scene and the clearly defined opposition of Rome and Orthodoxy. We find problems because we have got ordination wrong. Alan Richardson saw this clearly. 'To admit women to the priesthood would leave the present unsatisfactory situation exactly where it is, and would do nothing to promote the development of a wide variety of ministries which is the church's most immediate need'.[2]

The whole question becomes defused if we see ordination not in terms of a threefold hierarchy but in the broader understanding of a shared and multiple local leadership such as prevailed in the corporate presbyterate of the early church. Once we recover that, the problem shrinks to very small proportions. Women as well as men may well show that they have been given the charism of leadership. The church will appropriately recognise this by ordination. Women will then take their place alongside men within the local presbyterate. I believe that the creation pattern and the New Testament emphasis on the supportive role in ministry to be exercised by women might be best retained if the leadership of such a mixed team were normally, if not invariably, in the hands of a man. But perhaps I am unable sufficiently to extricate myself from my own cultural heritage and that of the New Testament! The debate would doubtless continue on the appropriateness of overall female leadership in a mixed team. But I can see no reason why a woman should not preside at the Eucharist as naturally as she would exercise the other leadership roles with which God has endowed her. Women already exercise many of these gifts within the Anglican communion. In some parts they are ordained priest; in all parts you may find them as readers, missionaries, parish workers, deacons. We have either already gone too far or not far enough. If women may at present teach and preach and evangelise, and sometimes baptise, why on earth should they not preside at the Lord's table? With their orders of deacons and widows, with their assertion that in Christ male and female are equal, the early Christians were in the forefront of contemporary thought. Can the same be said of us today? Michael Harper's *Let My People Grow* and the Grove Booklet *Evangelicals and the Ordination of Women* give some of the reasons that underlie the Church of England's synodical assertion that there is no theological objection to the ordination of women, with the rider that the time is not ripe to do anything about it! The question arouses such passion largely because ordination is misconceived; many think of priestesses and female bishops with misgiving. But once we get ordination right as a group of local presbyters working together in leadership, the problem of a woman's ordination is very nearly resolved. In such a team women's full participation and men's overall leadership (if that is right) could equally be preserved.

For the last ten years I have worked in such a team, so I know its value. First as principal of a theological seminary with a dozen or so on the staff, male and female, sharing a corporate oversight. Women members of the team could do anything a man could do, with one exception, and they did many things a good deal better. The one exception was of course celebrating the Eucharist, which in obedience to the canons of the Church of England was not open to them any more than it was to male lay members of staff.

More recently I have had the privilege to be rector of a parish with an equally shared ministry, male and female, ordained and lay: about fourteen of us are on the full-time staff team. Once again the lady members of the team have done anything the rest of the men have done, apart from celebrating the Eucharist. It is only out of deference to the canon law of the Church of England that they do not do that. In all other ways they are taking their place as full and highly valued members of the team. Such partnership is theologically sound and practically effective. It has a lot to offer to any local church. And much of it can be implemented even before there is a repeal of the Act of Uniformity.

CHAPTER NINE

CALLING AND TRAINING

I propose to end this book with two chapters of a more practical nature. The first arises from many years working in a theological college, where our task was to prepare men for ministry. The second arises from some years of practical ministry in a team situation at the heart of Oxford.

What should we look for in leaders?

We have already looked at the role of local leadership in general terms. Let us recapitulate, and add a little. Not all the following gifts will be found in any one member, which makes a shared ministry so important. But they are all requisite in the leadership of a local church.

1. *Leaders should be called.* In the Old Testament priesthood 'one does not take the honour upon himself, but he is called by God' (Heb. 5:4). This quality is no less essential to New Testament leadership. The candidate, those who train and examine him, and the church at large need to be sure of this first important issue: is there a genuine call? If there is, it will show itself one way or another. People will realise it. It will survive hard times, delays and disappointment.

2. *Leaders should be examples.* Paul said time and again 'I have showed you', 'I have given you an example', 'What you have learned and received and seen in me do', and the like. If the minister's life is not eloquent for his cause, nobody will listen to his words.

3. *Leaders should be corporate*. They must not play the one-man-priest. If they do, they will not only be flying in the face of the New Testament ideal of a corporate presbyterate, but will find themselves doing all sorts of things they were never intended to, and will be likely to rob others of their God-given place and function within the Body.

4. *Leaders should be enablers*. They must see their task to build up the saints for their work of service (Eph. 4:12). They must not try to do it all themselves, but endeavour to make themselves unnecessary because they delight to step into the background as others discover their gifts and begin to use them for the good of the Body.

5. *Leaders should be able to evangelise*. They may not be evangelists by gifts and inclination, but like Timothy must 'do the work of an evangelist' (2 Tim. 4:5). Christians are committed to the good-news business, and it is necessary for their leaders to be in it up to the hilt.

6. *Leaders should be able to preach*. A minister must 'herald' the gospel: that is precisely the word so often used in the New Testament. If he cannot preach, and is not prepared to allow others to do so, there is sure to be a drift away from the church.

7. *Leaders should be able to teach*. That is a requirement heavily stressed in the Pastoral Epistles. This again does not mean that the leaders must do it all themselves. It certainly does not mean that they must do it all by talking. But by encouraging private study, by helping group leaders to function, by holding debates, by using film, reading and study material, ministers must see that learning and growth in the understanding and practice of the faith go on in the congregation and in their own lives. That is going to require study of the scriptures and of the modern world as well (2 Tim. 2:15). It is going to necessitate doing battle for the truth and confronting error. All this will neither be easy nor popular, yet it must be done (1 Tim. 4, 2 Tim. 3).

8. *Leaders should be able to shepherd*. They need to care for others. This may not be the particular talent of every individual leader, but they must see that it is done. They are called to be undershepherds in the flock, and they must discharge that responsibility (1 Pet. 5:1–5). Social concern, pastoral counselling, visiting, building up, helping people to discover their gifts – all this and much more is involved.

9. *Leaders should be able to lead*. They are called to 'bear rule' to 'stand out in front' (1 Thess. 5:12,13; Rom. 12:8). They must be able to initiate the action after catching the vision; to take risks, to encourage the congregation to bold, courageous, costly action. This is going to demand character, and decisiveness, and the ability to stimulate (and if necessary be restrained by) fellow leaders. It will involve 'up front' work in leadership of the services, of the committees and of the whole church. Leaders must lead. They may often do so from behind, like the officers in the Royal Artillery! But lead they must.

10. *Leaders should be tested*. These nine points stand out clearly in the New Testament as requirements in those who are going to exercise leadership. Is it any wonder that Paul adds a tenth, the insistence that a young man, an untried person, should not be thrown into leadership too soon? He must have had some experience. He must have given proof that God has indeed equipped him with ministerial gifts. 'He must not be a recent convert . . .' says the wise old apostle. 'Let them also be tested first . . .' (1 Tim. 3.6,10).

What are the tests of vocation?

The social context

Begin by glancing at the shape of the society in which the Christian is called to serve. In the world at large we can expect to see the growing impact of factors which are even now gnawing away at society: overpopulation; famine on an ever-increasing scale; developing tension between the 'haves' and the 'have-nots', both within countries and between them; the diminution of non-renewable natural resources; the accelerating destruction of our environment; the terrifying and escalating nuclear threat; and technology racing out of control.[1] In addition we shall see an increasing lack of purpose in many lives as unemployment grows and the silicon chip makes its revolution in industry. Unless we learn how to use leisure and how to relate to people better than we have ever done before, there is little hope for the world.

Moreover, we may expect to see a decline of organised religion, a growth in religious pluralism, an increasing suspicion of enthusiasm, and a relativistic concept of truth. Crime, corruption, and tension between sectors in society are all on the increase and are sure to grow. Man's greed has not diminished. Aimlessness is prevalent. Privatisation is on the increase. Hedonism is the prevailing philosophy. Suicide and despair are round the corner. There is no rock on which to build. This is the type of society in which a great many Western Christians are called to serve.

The ecclesiastical context

And the church, what is the climate there? There will be far fewer clergy, as funds to support them crumble away in the surge of inflation. There will be an increase of self-supporting ministries which make no financial charge on congregations. The established churches will probably go broke. The Church of England will transform, or die. House fellowships may take over where empty parish churches leave off, and catholicity will be threatened. Clerical security of tenure will be a thing of the past. No longer will a clergyman be able to count it his right to be paid. Lay ministry is bound to increase. Naturally, therefore, lay training will become crucial. But as yet there is no sign of much awareness in top church leadership that this is a priority. Few dioceses invest money and manpower in a programme of serious lay training.

We are living in a time of faster change than ever before. In the next quarter of a century the following developments in church life are highly probable. Some parishes will continue to exist, with their paid full-time staff as before; but they will be few. Cathedrals may be taken over by the State. A great many churches will be closed through lack of interest and financial support to keep them going. The Church of England may well be disestablished. At all events it is likely to come under ever more severe financial pressure. During the past three years the contributions of St. Aldate's parish to the Diocese of Oxford have gone up by over 350%: this cannot continue. There is likely to be a complete financial breakdown in the established church as we know it.

This need be no disaster. It might drive us back towards New Testament principles in a way that theological considerations have failed to do. Unless we make radical changes, we shall be faced increasingly with a circuit ministry, as one clergyman seeks to serve a dozen local churches. This will be combined with an almost total lack of pastoral oversight. Specialised ministerial teams will develop, especially in inner city areas. The majority of church leaders will earn their money from a secular job and will be non-stipendiary clergy. There will have to be a great flowering of lay leadership if the church is to survive. And it is not impossible even in England that a communist or humanist takeover of power could bring the Church as an institution to a close.

Considerations for the assessors

In testing vocations for ministry in such a world, and such a church, here are some appropriate questions for the bishops' selectors and principals of theological colleges.

1. *Is he a man of God?* Only a genuinely converted man, deeply committed to Christ, with a strong devotional life, is going to survive and cut ice in an increasingly hostile and unsympathetic environment.

2. *What of his life?* Titus 1 and 1 Timothy 3 give shrewd and stringent criteria here. Questions like this arise: Is he overconfident? Is he quick tempered? Is he a one-woman

man? Is he over-keen on drink? Is he able to control himself and organise his family life? Is he unduly keen on his pay? Has he got an open home? Is he well recommended by churchmen and non-Christians alike? These questions all emerge from Titus 1.7ff. That same Epistle prompts others: Is he honest about his failures (Titus 3:3)? Is he likely to help in cases of need (Titus 3:14)? Is he prepared to engage in controversy for the faith, gently but firmly, and without personal bitterness (Titus 1:11; 3:2)? Is he discerning (Titus 3:9)? Unless a man's life passes scrutiny his ministry is bound to be ineffective.

3. *Can he work in a team?* Such teams of ministry are going to become more and more crucial. Is he basically a prima donna, seeking a stage to play on? Or will he be a team member, and be able to co-operate with other ministers, both male and female, other denominations, other theological positions?

4. *Can he communicate?* Has he learnt, in this media age, the way to communicate something of importance to those who have no idea of its importance? Can he detach himself from time-honoured language and imagery, from ecclesiastical assumptions and ways, and communicate the faith to those outside it? Can he write in an attractive way? Can he draw a crowd in the open air? Can he relate to folk in a deprived or multinational area?

5. *Does he like people?* If not, he is going to be no use in the shepherd ministry. The learned recluse, the pompous parson is going to be of little value in the next twenty years. People are needed who will go out among a very needy humanity and get deeply involved.

6. *What of his intellectual capacity?* I do not look for brilliance or a good degree. I look for the ability to teach. That is the prime condition, other than a holy life, which we find in the Pastoral Epistles. A man must be *didaktikos*, apt to teach (Titus 1:9; 1 Tim. 3:2). Alas, many clergy are totally inept at teaching. They have little understanding of

how people learn, and little sense of the urgency of
teaching the faith. Just ask yourself how much effective
training goes on in your church! If the candidate is to be apt
to teach, he must also be apt to learn. He must be a thinker,
and must be prepared to study. He needs to be in some
measure a theological resource man.

7. *Is he flexible?* Many men are intransigent on
peripheral matters, but soft at the centre. He should be the
reverse. In a fast-changing social climate flexibility is
essential; so is tenacious commitment to the faith. It is this
skilled adaptability that is so rare and so necessary. The
Church at large has failed signally here. Either clergy have
been avant-garde and distanced themselves from the
historic faith, or else they have stuck punctiliously and
unimaginatively to the way it was expressed in previous
generations.

8. *Has he got vision?* Particularly, he needs a vision of
the Body of Christ in a given area, with every member
working properly. Has he the determination to see this
vision carried through into reality? Is he likely to be sensitive to perceive new needs and new opportunities as they
arise? Or is he an 'as it was in the beginning, is now, and
ever shall be' man?

9. *Is he prepared to sacrifice?* He will be called to this in
the area of money, time, family, ambitions and probably
persecution. If he is weak on sacrifice he is going to be weak
on the servant ministry, which is the only ministry worth
having in the church of the Servant.

Questions for the candidate

So much for testing vocation from the point of view of those
called to train. What are the indications for the possible
candidate? How can he begin to sense the call of God in this
matter?

1. *He must be willing to do anything*. It must be 'Teach

me thy way, O Lord,' not 'Bless my way, O Lord' (Ps. 27:11). Only when we are totally open to God's guidance can we expect to receive it.

2. *He would be wise to expose himself to a variety of circumstances*, so as to see and develop gifts which at present he may have no idea he has. God does use circumstances to guide us (Acts 16:9,10).

3. *He must examine the scriptures*. Not so much for proof texts, though on occasion God can and does guide by illuminating some particular verse. But the general thrust of scripture can be of enormous value in disciplining and directing his thought processes, so that he begins to have the mind of Christ and think as Christ would think about contemporary issues, including his calling.

4. *He must assess his capabilities*. Charles Spurgeon had a wise saying: 'If God calls a man to be a preacher he gives him a big chest!' In other words, where God calls he equips. If God is calling him to leadership in the church, then there will already be some indications in the way he is blessing the man's ministry at present. Incipient gifts of ministry will be evident in his life.

5. *He should consult others*. Not that others are necessarily right, but if it is God's will that he should exercise ministry in the congregation it is probable that others will have noted the possibility too and will encourage him to press ahead and knock on the door to see if it opens.

6. *He should consult his own heart's longings*. God is not an ogre. He delights to 'give you the desires of your heart' (Ps. 37:4). Let him not make the mistake of supposing that if he wants to do a thing it cannot possibly be the will of God.

7. *He should expect a growing inner conviction*. If it is a real call from God it will survive the douche of cold water, the ecclesiastical delays, the problems along the way. It will

welcome tests as confirmations, or the reverse, of what has
seemed to be a call.

Those are some of the considerations to bear in mind
when considering whether or not God is calling us to a
ministry of leadership in the church. We should beware of
dogmatic utterances from others; of impulse in ourselves;
of supposing that in this very needy world the recognition
of need necessarily constitutes the call of God. It does not.
There is need everywhere. What matters is that between
them the candidate, the local church and the wider leadership of the church of God come to a common mind about
where and how this particular limb within the Body
of Christ should find his or her main sphere of
service.

How shall we train for ministry?

All Christians are called to serve their Lord, the church,
each other, and society. Once this basic biblical truth
begins to be believed, taught and acted upon, ecclesiastical
hearts will beat less irregularly at the rise and fall of
numbers offering for 'the ministry'. Leaders will emerge in
each local area, and be recognised by the church through
ordination. Some of these will probably be trained locally
on the job. Others will continue, as at present, to have at
least part of their training in a residential college. Some will
derive their income from continuing in secular work.
Others, particularly those with special gifts which cry out to
be used more widely than in a single congregation, may
well be paid as full-time workers. But the day of appealing
for vocations to *the* ministry will have ended. Instead will
come steady teaching in each congregation to encourage
every member to seek God's call for the area of work within
which to exercise most effectively and usefully the charism
God has bestowed.

The variety of leadership which the New Testament
leads us to envisage in a healthy church sets a high
premium on training. This the Church of England has
handled with such an obvious double standard that its real
assumptions about ministry are painfully obvious. In the

year in which I write the Church is spending over a million pounds on the equipping of a few hundred ordinands. At the same time, a derisory sum is being spent on lay training. Yet more and more parishes are grouped frenetically into larger and larger units, and fewer and fewer stipendiary clergy circulate in ever faster circles. It seems to me, therefore, that we are called to consider training of three types.

Training local presbyters

First, we must train local presbyters. These will, if we follow the New Testament, be tried people of experience. They will be men and women who have shown gifts of ministry: some administrative, some teaching, some counselling, some evangelistic. Together a group of them will be able to constitute an effective all-round corporate presbyterate. They might fittingly be ordained by the bishop once he is satisfied of their competence to lead in the local situation.

This competence is partly gained by book learning, but it is gained much more from experience. This is where the value of shared ministry shows itself. Within the corporate presbyterate there will be many skills on offer. New candidates will learn a great deal by apprenticeship to more experienced colleagues. That, after all, is how the church has trained its ministers down the years. The Timothys got trained by the Pauls, not by taking them away and putting them in colleges. There is a great value in college life, but it is not best fitted for training local leaders for practical ministry.

The local presbyterate will naturally meet regularly: probably early in the morning, if many of them have secular jobs. This team will learn from one another and from scripture, from experience, from the occasional presence of some Christian leader from another part of the country or the world who happens to be in town.

Some at least of the training could be in co-operation with a local theological college or even a university department. I foresee a great increase of theological education by extension, which has proved so valuable in Latin America and India. This means that the college comes to the candidates, not vice versa. One or more central experts, from a college or elsewhere, come to train local leaders on the spot.

With the growing sophistication and decreasing cost of television we can look forward not only to high calibre teaching being filmed on video and played from cassettes, but to the possibility, already happening in Christian education in America, of having the teachers available for questioning by pupils on television, by means of satellite. The development of the silicon chip means that the next twenty years are likely to be even more revolutionary in the area of audio-visuals than the previous twenty years have been. Is the church at large going to wake up to the enormous possibilities of widespread Christian education which technical advances have made possible? Or will it, ostrich-like, continue to depend on the preaching and teaching gifts of the one local pastor, who may well himself have had little training in this vital area of Christian communication?

However, once the need for training is seen, and the facilities grasped, the local situation, weak as it currently is, could be transformed in a few years. Through reading, through courses held in the local church, city wide, and on T.V., Christians could grow in understanding. By practical involvement in local ministry, and sometimes by going out in teams to visit other churches, the budding local leadership could be 'earthed' and equipped for useful service.

Jesus trained his followers by apprenticeship. They *saw* him work, then *shared* in his work, then *did* it themselves, then *trained* others. The church greatly needs to recover this pattern of training a group of leaders in each congregation. Among other benefits, there would no longer be the hiccups and policy changes associated in many a parish with the arrival of a new vicar. Instead there would be the gradual development of a leadership team, able to offer more effective and stable all round ministry in the church; able also to survive the departure of a vicar without hiatus.

Whether or not ordination to the local presbyterate should continue to be for life would, no doubt, be hotly contested. If not, the authorisation could be for a limited and renewable period. If a lifelong concept of ordination continued, there would be need for a strict exercise of the diocesan licence to officiate. This would enable any mistakes to be rectified, and would also mean that if a presbyter in one area went to another where he had not yet earned the right to lead, his presbytership would not be exercised in practice, unless and until the call came from that particular church to join their team and he was licensed. Needless to say, this local training and equipping of new presbyters through membership of a corporate body would be infinitely cheaper than our present expensive and élitist method of training.

Lay training

Second, we must concentrate on lay training. I do not like the word, for reasons expressed above. There are not two classes within the church. All are called to serve. And that is just what these lay training courses must show. Congregations do need training to see themselves as the Body of Christ, where all are expected to contribute to the whole such gifts as God has entrusted to each. There needs to be training in the faith, training for new converts, training in marriage and parenthood, training for different areas of ministry within the church. A comprehensive scheme of Christian education needs to be undertaken regularly.

It may well be that despite the different church habits in Britain our congregation could adapt and greatly profit by the all-age Sunday School which is a feature of American Christianity. This means that a series of courses is provided, and members of the congregation go not only to the worship service but to one of these courses as well. Certainly the standard of Christian education in most British congregations is deplorably low. The average Christian today probably knows less about his faith than the reasonably competent Sunday scholar half a century ago.

Naturally, the local presbyters will receive this education as well as being among the dispensers of it. This is worlds away from the current supposition that the clergy know it all (or are supposed to know it all) already. They do not. There are members of congregations who have specialist skills to teach in the local church – skills in counselling, ethics, science and religion to which most clergy are comparative strangers. These resources urgently need to be tapped.

There is need for a wide spectrum of continuous Christian education in the local church: in country areas, this could be done at deanery or market-town level and preferably interdenominationally. As members of the congregation get into these training courses, begin to relish them and learn from them, they will discover and use their gifts. The result will be a growing number within the local church of people who are using their talents for the Lord, and thus a growing cadre of potential presbyters for the future. If a massive education scheme like this is to be undertaken (and it is crucial) then dioceses will need to finance it, and themselves have the humility to learn how it can be done effectively. There will need to be new attitudes in the pew and among the clergy. But it can be done. In places it is being done. When it is done, the church comes alive.

College training

The third training area is, of course, the theological colleges. These have been pruned in recent years, and those which remain are now offering a better training than previously. All college staffs know the problems and the strains. The curriculum keeps increasing while nothing offers to drop out! The training, being residential, is inevitably more academic and less practical than would be desirable. The academic aspect therefore assumes more importance in the minds of staff and students alike because it is more readily assessable. At present it is very hard to 'fail' the unsatisfactory student if he has negotiated his selection precedure and manages to pass his academic exams. Ordination is seen as the carrot to encourage the student along the road. All of these things, and many others, add to the frustrations of a theological college teacher.

But if most of the local presbyters were trained on the ground a good many of these problems would disappear. The college would continue to be of the utmost importance. It would be the place where the most rigorous examination of every side of the faith and life of the church took place. It would be the place where some of the local presbyters would undergo short or longer course training for special purposes. It would have a small number of young men taking honours and advanced degrees with a view to becoming the scholars and academic leaders of the church in the next generation. Its staff would themselves become a corporate leadership which could offer a model to others throughout the area. They would at certain periods of the year run refresher courses and at others go out to offer theological education by extension courses.

It is the colleges, rather than the universities, which need to become the seedbed for the intellectual leadership of the church. Universities are increasingly setting up departments in the phenomenology of religion, and moving away from departments in Christian theology. That move will accelerate under the influences at work in our society, and the church must react accordingly, by placing less and less reliance on university departments for the training of church leadership, and also by encouraging the most able students to devote their skills not to writing doctorates on minutiae which are of little significance to the church, but to building up the leadership of the next generation. And what could be more worthwhile than that?

Such a use of theological college resources and personnel would enable the staff to have a much greater contact with and influence on the life of the churches at local level. It would make a far greater use of their gifts and expertise which would be made available, through extension courses, to far more people. The college would be used for short-term as well as long-term candidates, with ordination no longer being the inevitable goal. For the training would not be for the untried, but rather for the further equipping of those who have already received some training at local level, and are already displaying gifts of leadership in the local church.

These are some of the ways in which theological training in the future could better serve the corporate local leadership of the church of the Servant. The question is, will we dare to be radical enough while there is still time?

CHAPTER TEN

BUILDING FOR SERVICE

Scholars have often discussed why the twenty-first chapter of the Gospel of St. John was added to what seems to be a completed book. After the confession of Thomas and the words of encouragement uttered by Jesus to those who have not seen and yet have believed, it is surprising that a further chapter ensues: there is almost a sense of anti-climax.

It is perfectly possible that the Gospel at first circulated without chapter twenty-one. But it was soon added, and almost certainly by the same author with the commendation and encouragement of his Christian friends ('we know that his testimony is true' John 21:24). Why was it thought necessary?

Partly, no doubt, to show Peter's triple reinstatement by Jesus after his triple denial. Partly, possibly, because it was necessary to counter rumours that the 'beloved disciple' had been told by Jesus that he would not die but survive until the parousia. But surely the main purpose of the chapter is to show the threefold task of the church that Christ left behind to carry on his work. They must catch fish (vv.1-14) and they must feed sheep (v.15ff). The making of disciples and the training of disciples are the two major aspects of the ministry of Christ in the world. The role of leaders is the third strand in this chapter which is inseparable from the other two: they must be both partners and enablers.

We have looked at the theory of Christian ministry a good deal in the previous chapters of this book. Now I propose, diffidently, to show how we are attempting to carry out those principles in one parish, and that in many ways a very peculiar one. I write from the heart of Oxford, from a church where half of the congregation are undergraduates, who are only in residence for just over half the year. Very few families, problems of the inner city, international residents, antiquated buildings – these are some of its characteristics. It is by no stretch of imagination a typical parish, and the way in which the principles of ministry enunciated above are worked out will certainly be very different in other parts of the country and in different social settings. Nevertheless the principles themselves have withstood a good deal of testing down the years: evangelism, training, body life, shared leadership, are four principles of ministry which can and should be applied anywhere. But I write diffidently, because our church has a long way to go. We have not by any means achieved all that we want to, and we make many mistakes. Nevertheless, unless a book such as this is grounded in experience it is very easy to dismiss the principles as unrealistic, or at all events incapable of application within the structures of the Church of England.

The making of disciples

If the church genuinely does exist for the benefit of those who are not yet its members, strenuous efforts must be made to reach them. The church at large has a bad image, and this assuredly will not be overcome if congregations continue the way they are. A definite initiative is required.

1. *First comes the ministry of prayer*. Without that, nothing happens. Unless we are praying for people to come to the Lord, praying regularly and corporately and imaginatively and in faith, we shall not see very much. Therefore a parish prayer meeting of some sort is a necessity. It may happen in silence. It may happen by prayer in groups. It may happen at a central prayer meeting. It may involve prayer breakfasts, prayer partnerships, nights of prayer. But the ministry of prayer is clearly crucial for the growth and deepening of any church.

2. *The church must be seen to care.* So often it appears as a private hobby. Like a gardening club the church seems to be a society bent on its own preservation, but without paying much attention to others. Yet if it is to cut any ice, it must be seen to care about the quality of life in the area and the problems folk wrestle with. For instance, it may need to contend for the supply of playgroups, or fair shares for racial minorities in such employment as is available. It may start, and staff, an adoption clinic, as an alternative to the evil of abortion. Whatever the problems that affect the life of the community, the church needs to be seen to care for the good of those who are not its members: Jesus did.

Unemployment is one of the scourges of our day. The church needs to be seen to be concerned, and involved. It may launch a job creation scheme. It may run a coffee bar for disenchanted youth. It may initiate a night shelter for homeless teenagers. It may be involved in the housing of those with nowhere to go. It may bring into being a restaurant or coffee house where people can rest and eat, be surprised at the quality of food and love – and then discover it is run by the church. Care shows itself in a thousand ways. Unless it does, however, evangelism will prove fruitless.

3. *The church must be a friendly place.* The average public house is much more friendly than the average church. Churchmen underestimate the fear and prejudice against even entering a church building which inhibits millions in this country. Therefore friendship is the great way of breaking down barriers and demonstrating the Servant ministry. A simple expedient like having people greet one another for a five-minute 'buzz' at the start of the service; the serving of coffee afterwards; the ready invitations for visitors to have a meal or spend a night – these things make a profound impact, the more so because, to our shame, they are generally unexpected. In the case of students, Christians at Oxford University write to every single freshman and woman before they come up to the university. They offer friendship and invite them, if they wish, to the Christian fellowship. Many new students are

met by Christians as they arrive, and are helped to settle in. Several of the churches offer a free lunch to all new students at the university. In ways like this a seed is sown – if only of curiosity.

4. *Evangelistic preaching in church* is something which every church could and should do at appropriate times in the year. If there is any regular turnover in the congregation, it is a fair assumption that some at least will not have a personal Christian faith, but will be visiting the church in a spirit of enquiry or mild interest. On three or four occasions in the year we have a well-prepared, well-advertised evangelistic address which is designed unashamedly to help people to repentance and faith in Christ. The worship, the music, the employment of appropriate aids such as dance, drama, banners and testimony may be useful, and they are all subordinated to the one aim of drawing men and women to Christ. At the end of the service an opportunity is given for those who so wish to stay behind and entrust their lives to Christ. They are interviewed within the next twenty-four hours and directed into groups for new Christians.

5. *Evangelism outside church.* Evangelism need not be confined to set pieces in church. We find that other settings are often preferable. We have engaged in it at supper parties in people's homes: after the meal there is an opportunity to give an arresting talk on some aspect of the faith and take comments, criticisms and questions from those present. This often is very fruitful, particularly if the party has a certain homogeneity — sportsmen, for instance, or young couples. A major enterprise, carefully planned, using the Town Hall is another means of outreach. One could use a musical evening with a Christian artist who both sings and speaks about Christ; or a debate between a well known Christian and non-Christian; or a seasonal event such as a pre-Christmas multi-media presentation. The value of high quality slide-tape sequences is considerable; there is often someone in the congregation who can take good pictures and one or two others who can arrange the

sound and the production. Often very short sequences have a great impact. In the Oxford colleges it is often possible to respond to invitations to speak in somebody's rooms or a lecture hall; better still in the college bar, with the assistance of some dramatic sketches and testimony from the students in that college. A recent summer development in Oxford which proved very fruitful was an evangelistic strawberry and Pimms' party in a college garden, complete with music to match! There is no end to the ways in which the gospel can be shared, naturally and without embarrassment, if we have the imagination and motivation to get involved.

6. *Debates have their place, too.* All too often the Christian case is insulated from come-back because of the privileged position given to the sermon. But if it *is* the truth of God, it can withstand confrontation and opposition. I have found that a debate with a leading secularist on the nature of man, or with students on free sex, or with communists on goals for society, or in a debating society on the evidence for the resurrection of Jesus – these things all draw a crowd, composed largely of those who would not go to normal Christian gatherings. Sometimes people discover Christ through only one such presentation. More often they are set on the trail of enquiry: reading, arguing, and thinking, which can in due course lead them to faith.

7. *Open-air ministry* is generally thought to have had its day, at least in fairly sophisticated locations. This could not be further from the truth. Wesley and Whitefield changed the face of England through open-air preaching in the eighteenth century. We find that the presentation of the Christian message in the open air remains both enjoyable and effective in the twentieth. Not, of course, if it is delivered by a mournful man at a street corner exhorting his hearers to repent and meet their God! But if a large group gathers in a well-populated place – a high street, a shopping precinct, a beach – and proceeds with humour and joy to speak of Christ inductively, taking a cue from the situation prevailing at the time, it can cause great interest.

People don't expect it. They imagine that Christians will keep to their churches. But if we have good news, why should we stay confined to our buildings? Jesus was an open-air preacher; why should his followers not be?

Three factors help enormously in open-air work. The first is dance. We use Israeli group dances in the streets and this amazes people. 'What have these people got to be so happy about?' is their question, spoken or unspoken. Once that question is lodged in their minds, the speaker's task is made so much easier. He has simply to tell them what accounts for this joy. Equally, short dramatic sketches often seem to get through to places where the ordinary spoken word does not reach. They are a most powerful medium, and if some of the congregation see it as their Christian ministry to write and rehearse such playlets, it will be of great value for the spread of the gospel. A third asset is the use of visual material. Jesus preached continually from the things all around him, and used them as vehicles to draw people to God. We can do the same, and we should. A particularly effective way to do this is by means of a sketch board. It immediately draws a crowd, and those who are really interested stay on for personal conversation.

Always the most valuable part of the open-air work is the conversations which begin round the edge of the crowd. These often ripen into something more, and lead to interest and sometimes to conversion. Even when things do not go that far, a nice taste in the mouth is left behind: people see that the church can come out from behind its fortifications, that it is not dull, but is comprehensible and happy. If that impression has been created, time has not been wasted.

8. *A period of mission.* This can take many forms. It may be a weekend of Christian apologetics and evangelistic preaching put on by some church either in its own building or on common ground. It may be a full week-long event, carefully prepared for over a period of time. We engage each September in a fortnight of mission with a church or series of churches in a town, taking a team of 80-100 with us. They do not all preach, of course: many of them are

young and inexperienced Christians. But their common life, their love for Christ, their willingness to have a go, their imagination and hard work speedily endear them to the local Christians who are encouraged and stimulated. The Body is seen to be operating in every part, and in love. There are house meetings, much visiting, teaching in schools, factory visits, entry into prisons and borstals, and of course central meetings and youth events, together with preaching and speaking at all levels in the churches on Sundays. In ways like this many people come to a living faith, and this is as much encouragement to the visitors as it is to the local Christians. The shared enterprise of mission brings fellowship and much joy.

9. *Personal evangelism*. At the other end of the spectrum from a public event like the large mission, personal evangelism is almost a hidden ministry. Here one friend takes another friend to church or a meeting – or they simply find themselves talking about the things of God. If members of the congregation have been schooled in how to lead another to faith, there will be enough basic knowledge there for the Holy Spirit to use. We certainly find that a good many people each year come to Christ through the personal conversations they have had with one or more Christian friends; this is a more effective method than preaching or big meetings, because it enables the enquirer to come out with what is really bothering him and proving an obstacle to faith. In the first chapter of St. John Jesus himself led a string of individuals to faith in this way, by personal and very natural conversation. It is a ministry to be coveted, and training needs to be offered within the congregation. Then there will not be undue reliance on the ministry of the 'professional'; ordinary church members will find to their great delight what a privilege it is to lead someone else to the feet of Jesus. They will then have a great zest to do it again!

The training of disciples

Believers in Christ embark on a life of obedience.

Some evangelists too readily forget that Christ calls men not so much to decision as to discipleship. How is a church to conserve and build up the results of its outreach?

1. *Agnostics' Groups.* Perhaps we would do well to begin one stage further back. In our church we find it useful to arrange small groups for people who are unsure about the Christian faith and are prepared to consider the evidence. Sometimes these Agnostics' Groups are run by one or two experienced Christians and, say, ten agnostics; sometimes on a fifty-fifty basis. Sometimes the group works out its own agenda, sometimes it goes through a book like C.S. Lewis's *Mere Christianity,* or tackles basic issues, one each week. The purpose of the group is to help members discover their way to Christ by removing difficulties and objections along the route. This requires understanding, patience and empathy. It is important to expose people to scripture, which has its own power, even when folk profess not to believe it. A meal and friendship are important ingredients in forming trust and promoting openness. The loan of books on different aspects of Christian faith and behaviour can help; so can the companionship of other Christians and the testimony of those who have recently been agnostics themselves.

Such groups ought to be a common feature in the churches of our land, but in my experience they are rather rare. Why so? The clergyman is supposed to be trained in the content of the faith and other world views; this should be the sort of group in which he might be expected to excel. But it may be that other members of the congregation have greater gifts in this particular and exacting ministry. No matter by whom, this is something that needs to be done on a widespread scale in a post-Christian country like Britain. The non-Christian is not going to come to a church; the church must come to him. Christians must engage him in open discussion in home or pub. It is hard work, but very rewarding. We find that a good half of those who commit themselves to this eight-week course of enquiry in an agnostics' group become Christians before the end of the course.

2. *Beginners' Groups.* From the Agnostics' Group or from personal or churchbased evangelism, the Beginners' Groups are stocked. Our own church depends heavily on these for the nurture of new believers. Our situation is peculiar in that we are set in the midst of a continually changing open-minded group of intelligent and enquiring young people: but every church that expects to win new believers needs to work out an appropriate means for their nurture. Coming to church is not enough: it will probably be a totally strange world for them, to begin with. Attachment to a church house-group will normally not be a good idea initially either. The new believer would start a long way behind the others, and be intimidated. He is full of doubts and questions, and needs careful and specialised attention. A Beginners' Group consists of two or three leaders and a dozen or so new believers (or those seeking a refresher course in Christian basics). Each week they examine some important area of the faith – assurance, prayer, the church, the Holy Spirit, the Bible, the person of Jesus, and so forth. The way in which each subject is handled will depend on the group. There may be an introductory talk; there may be a guided study. There may be a supper shared, a verse of scripture memorised. There will probably be a bookstall. There will certainly be a time of sharing of joys, discoveries and problems; and there will be a time of Bible reading in a small group followed by prayer. Each person shares what they find most helpful in the passage, and often the discussion is lively and highly relevant to life. They learn to pray, shortly and simply, at the end of each evening, though this may be a totally new experience to them. Notes are given out as they leave – and often it is midnight before they do!

They have learned so much even after one or two such evenings together. They have discovered Christian fellowship in the small group; they have found out that others have problems like themselves; they have found that the Bible speaks, and have begun to learn from it; they have gained insight into the theme of the evening; they have begun to pray in the company of others and discovered its joy and strange power for linking people in fellowship.

They have discovered that by their stumbling comments they help one another; they begin to make Christian friends in the group; they start the habit of verse learning and reading Christian books; they are no longer embarrassed to talk about their own spiritual discoveries and doubts. A great deal goes on in the dynamics of these small groups. In addition, the new Christian will need help with his own devotional life and with the worship and the behaviour of the Christian family into which he has come, so he will need one or two individual sessions with one of the leaders. He may well need to be baptised or confirmed, in due course. A weekend away for the group at the end of the course (which in our case lasts two months), is invaluable in binding folk together, and consolidating the work that has been done.

3. *Fellowship Groups*. Those graduating from Beginners' Groups are now ready for the basic cell structure that permeates the whole life of the church: we call them Fellowship Groups. Christians need the support not only of the large or formal church body, but also of the informal small group, preferably based on geographical location. In such a group each person is loved and valued. He learns to belong, and is missed if he is not there. These groups meet weekly or fortnightly, depending on the other structures within the church. Anything more infrequent than a fortnightly meeting is too little for the group to grow together in fellowship and real openness with one another. Ideally all members of the congregation will be part of one of these groups; in practice not more than half or three-quarters of them will.

These groups become the basic pastoral units in a church. The members do indeed bear one another's burdens and so fulfil the law of Christ. Problems are shared, joys celebrated, the scriptures studied and applied, and sometimes the group has a night out for recreation, or goes to paint some particular person's room as an act of love and fellowship. The members get to know and love and depend on one another. Close friendships develop. Several of our groups have extra breakfast meetings for prayer and companionship. And from time to time the whole group will go away for a weekend to relax, or for service in a church or mission situation. They become, in short, 'the church in the house' in these midweek gatherings, and 'the church gathered' on Sunday.

There are, of course, other groups in our church, but they all share in this 'Fellowship Group' concept. For instance there is a banner-making group, a dance group, a youth group, a women's meeting, a drama group, a choir group: but one and all are determined not only to engage in the particular activity which draws them together, but to adopt the role of the servant to one another, and so grow in partnership, love and unity. And this is one of the most attractive features of any Christian church; when its members manifestly love each other and the Lord very much. It shows. And it draws.

4. *Training Courses.* Training takes many forms, but a programme of continuous training is essential in a church that takes its servant commission seriously. Most churches have some form of training for confirmation, the baptism of adults, and the parents of candidates for infant baptism (though, scandalously, these are still by no means universal). But there it ends. The ignorant and willing are generally recruited for Sunday School teaching, but rarely trained! Christian education in the round is scarcely attempted in the Church of England, and the low standard of sermons, or rather, sermonettes, is not calculated to make for much growth. We need to take great pains with the training of one another in the congregation: we must build one another up.

The way in which our congregation attempts this training is somewhat as follows. From time to time we have training courses for various needs; for counselling, for marriage guidance and preparation; for mission; for leaders in youth work; for thinking in a Christian way. For the most part these groups are of short duration – up to ten weeks or so. But increasingly we have been discovering that a concentrated time away, be it a day, a weekend or a week is far more effective for training purposes than an extended course involving an evening a week.

Moreover, our Christian students in a particular discipline, whether politics or medicine, engineering or theology, tend to get together and discuss how their faith impinges on their academic discipline. This could just as effectively be done on the shop floor by Christian shop stewards, or by NCOs or officers in an army unit. In our particular congregation we have, during term time, a lunch on Sundays for those who like to come. Numbers are usually round 80–100. There is a chance to meet and greet new faces; there is the opportunity to quiz the preacher on his sermon and to take steps to apply it. This can be a real learning occasion, even though there is no formal teaching. It is part of training the church.

5. *Training for mission* ought to be included. Each year we take around a hundred members of the congregation – in our case mainly students – away for a two-week mission is some part of the country to which we have been invited by the local churches. The hosts have been engaged in preparatory house groups on an inter-church basis for a whole year. Such a mission is good for us. It enables our members to share in the spreading of the gospel and to see it taking root in new lives among ordinary people. And it is good for the parishes to which we go. They get drawn together ecumenically by the venture, and they receive converts after the mission is over. Naturally a mission like this requires us to train our members before we go, and this we attempt to do by an eight-week course and a preparatory visit to the town.

Recently we have seen the value of a public celebration of the Christian faith, bringing together all the churches in a town, and having a major focal point each night, along with street parties, open-air dance and drama, school visits and so forth. This enables a lot of teaching and mutual building up to take place; many barriers are broken down and inhibitions laid to rest. There is generally some evangelistic by-product as well.

A venture like this imparts something of the flavour of Christ to a whole town. While the 1981 Toxteth riots were going on in Liverpool, not far away, in Shipley, churches of all denominations joined with us in celebrating the faith for a week with large numbers, outdoor processions and great joy. 'Thanks be to God' wrote Paul in 2 Corinthians 2:14, 'who in Christ always leads us in triumph and through us spreads the fragrance of the knowledge of him everywhere.' That remains part of the church's calling, and it calls for training, though much is also spontaneous!

6. *Overall church training.* We try to do this in a variety of ways. One is by having carefully planned courses of sermons: sometimes topical, sometimes following the Church's year, sometimes expository. We try to be sensitive to what the needs are at the time. And recently we have learnt how foolish we were to dart from subject to subject each week. We need to go on teaching on a particular topic until it is learnt and acted upon. With this in mind we have just completed a nine-month course. We have been examining what it means to be an alternative society in a world that is falling apart. We have spent a whole month on each of nine aspects of this theme, and teaching has taken place at all levels in the church. We have preached on each topic for a whole month. The Fellowship Groups have discussed its application. The prayer meetings have centred round it. Slide-tape sequences have been produced on each topic. And we have made a loose-leaf guide book to the whole nine-month series, with opportunities for members to add material of their own.

The contents of this course may be of interest. The writer to the Hebrews shows how in a time when so much that seemed settled is being shaken, the church should exhibit qualities which belong to a lifestyle that cannot be shaken (Heb. 12:25–29). The marks of such a church are acceptable worship (12:28f, 13:15); love for the brethren (13:1); love for strangers (13:2) – which includes and should always accompany evangelism; love for the underprivileged (13:3); Christian family life (13:4); a simple lifestyle (13:5,6,16); spiritual leadership (13:7,17); sound teaching (13:9); and suffering (13:10–14)which is bound to be the badge of the faithful church, just as it was of the suffering Servant, her Lord.

The leadership of disciples

If a church is to engage in a servant ministry of mission and discipleship, this puts a great deal of responsibility upon the leadership. It is not surprising that in the New Testament Christian ministry is always shared ministry! No one man could or should undertake such an extensive ministry. It may be worth recounting how we have tried to go about building a leadership team.

The leadership of the church

The leadership in our particular church has three constituent parts. First there is the staff. Second there is the Parochial Church Council, and more especially its Standing Committee; and thirdly there is a small group of men and women in the church who have shown pastoral gifts and are designated as a group of lay pastors. This diversification has great value, though it sometimes takes a little time to pass a decision of importance through all three, especially since we look for a common mind led by the Lord, and eschew voting. But it means that there is a recognised pastoral group in the church to whom people can turn as well as to the clergy. It means that the leadership is shared between them on the pastoral side, and the P.C.C. on the worship and financial side, in addition to the ordained staff. And as some members are on two or, exceptionally, all three of those groups, it makes for cohesion.

Lay pastors

What, you may ask, are lay pastors? Members of the congregation whom God has clearly gifted for leadership in the church. What do they do? Each one has a responsibility for a few Fellowship Group leaders. He meets with them regularly to see how their groups are going, and to give encouragement and help as he is able. But the lay pastor has other responsibilities too. He often shares in the leading of worship; he may take the first part of the service, or lead the prayers, or speak. Some of the pastors have shown gifts of evangelism, some of training, and these are appreciated and used. We find that pastors will now take teams out to different churches in the vicinity, either to run a day conference embodying a number of seminars on different aspects of the faith, or to take services over a weekend. Occasionally one of them will go overseas with a team, in answer to an invitation. Sometimes a member of the ordained staff goes with such a group, but this is no longer necessary. The lay pastors are well able to excercise the leadership themselves. Is this not an indication of the type of training which would be invaluable for Auxiliary Pastoral Ministry and for Lay Readers within the Anglican Church? Would it not give that element of practical experience within a team of like-minded partners, which is at present so lacking in their largely bookish training? The church at large tends to make a big mistake with its men: they are generally given financial and administrative jobs. While these need to be done, it is important to involve men in the teaching, pastoral and evangelistic ministry of the church. In this way they develop fast, and the church develops with them.

We have found that it is imperative to keep the lay pastors in close contact both with the Fellowship Group leaders on the one hand and with the ordained staff on the other. Accordingly, we have been accustomed to meet for worship and breakfast fortnightly, and to have one evening a month as pastors and another as pastors and wives all together. In this way the pastors come very close to one another, and are able to share at a deep level; moreover they actually model that type of close fellowship which they hope to inculcate throughout the congregational groups which they oversee.

But where, you may ask, do these pastors spring from? The answer is simple. They are those who have shown pastoral gifts. When people display gifts of leadership and shepherding in the congregation they may well be called to this work. Some of them will have been Fellowship Group

leaders, but not all. Some will have displayed pastoral gifts
in other areas. By becoming pastors these people are
released from other responsibilities in the church and
enabled to use their gift for the Body as a whole.

They are set aside for this work in a service slightly
reminiscent of an ordination. Just as the bishop shares his
cure of souls with the incumbent, so the incumbent shares it
with them, publicly in the face of the congregation. We ask
pastors to serve for a renewable period of one year. Thus if
other work becomes pressing, if a wrong choice has been
made, or if the person moves away, the annual nature of
the appointment gives room for adjustment. We have tried
to follow the New Testament precedent of asking the congregation to suggest names, from which the existing leadership selects after prayerfully coming to a common mind.

Shared leadership

Leadership in New Testament days was shared. Whether
you look at the twelve apostles of Jesus, or the 'prophets
and teachers' in the church of Antioch (Acts 13:1), or the
five types of ministry characterised as Christ's gift to the
church (Eph. 4:11), the message is the same: Christian
leadership is both servant leadership and shared leadership. It abominates both domination and monarchy. But
monarchy is so much easier than shared leadership. There
is therefore a strong tendency for us to relapse into an
authoritarian stance when the pressures are on. How can
this be avoided, and shared leadership be made to work?
The following suggestions are not exhaustive, but they are
certainly rooted in experience – much of it painful.

1. *We must acknowledge the Lordship of Jesus.* That is to
say, we must recognise that the local church is not a
monarchy, to be run by the rector. It is not an oligarchy, to
be dominated by Parish Council or pastoral group. It is not
a democracy, to be controlled by the congregation at large.
The church is a theocracy. God created it, redeemed it,
owns and controls it. It is his will that we must seek and be
willing to follow. Therefore when we disagree on some

matter we must neither try to force our view on others, nor weakly give way to them. We must argue the case as clearly and forcibly as we can. We must then go away and pray; and go on praying until we come to a common mind. The way of the world is to vote. But that leaves a dissatisfied minority. The way of the Lord is to seek his face. When all want his will even more than their own ideas, he does make his way known. It may come through acceptance of the original majority view. It may come through recognition that the original minority view was right. It may come through some totally new insight. We have seen it come at times through a vision and at times through a prophetic message from one member which so had the ring of truth about it that all were convinced – and subsequent events showed the correctness of the decision. God will not guide us unless we deeply desire to go his way at all costs. In our church we have found that unitive guidance comes most readily after an extended period of worship and prayer. This could happen spontaneously in the course of a church business meeting – or perhaps during a special day given over to prayer and fasting and seeking the will of God for the church.

2. *We must listen to the church*. It is all too easy for the leadership of a church to get out of step with the membership. Instead of equipping the church members for their God-given ministries, the leadership pursues its own ideas. This can cause disunity and even disintegration in a congregation. But it can be avoided. We try to do this in two ways. First, we keep in constant touch with the feelings and priorities of church members through the Fellowship Group system. Each lay pastor relates to three or four Fellowship Group leaders, and meets them regularly. He also visits their groups from time to time. Two way communication is thus made easy. The other way is to have a shortened Sunday service occasionally, followed by a congregational discussion of some issue that is causing concern – and doing it within the context of worship, prayer, and openness. In ways such as these, together with the occasional questionnaire and written explanation of recent

decisions taken by the leadership, it is usually possible to
ensure that no substantial division emerges in the Body.
Often there may be truth on both sides of a controversial
issue, but the proportions have gone awry. Then the
guidance of the congregation at large can be of tremendous
value in restoring balance.

3. *We must recognise each other's gifts*. All leadership in
the church is a gift of Christ. Therefore we do well to
discern what those gifts are, in the leadership as well as in
the congregation as a whole, and set each person free to use
that gift for the good of the Body. 1 Corinthians 12:4–6 has
wise advice for us. We have all been baptised into the same
Body, and the Spirit of God has gifted every member. His
goals are diversity, but harmony. And three key words are
used by Paul to help the Corinthians understand their gifts.
The first is *charisma*: each member has received some
gracious endowment by the Lord. These are varied, and
not subject to human manipulation. The second word is
diakonia: the gifts are not intended for show but for
service. They are meant to build up the Body in some
appropriate way. The third word is *energema*: these gifts
should be exercised not in our strength but the Lord's. That
is how God's gifts are meant to fuse together for the good of
the whole Body.

If we accept this, it will have costly consequences. It
will mean that the vicar may not do all the preaching – or
even most of it, if he has not been particularly gifted as a
teacher, and others have been. He may have to yield to
others in evangelism, or administration, or counselling. My
wife is a much better counsellor than I: so she takes the lead
in this area of our ministry. Some of my colleagues are
much better at planning worship, chairing meetings, looking after the staff team than I. So they do it. I am ultimately
accountable to the congregation and to the bishop for the
way these matters are handled: the buck stops on my desk.
But this does not mean that I attempt to head up the various
aspects of our church's life. In most cases I work *under*
some other member of the team (over which I preside)
because God has manifestly gifted him or her more than me

in that area. Ministry is, after all, a matter of function, not
of status. But we will still find that a hard lesson to master: at
least, I do! Yet how worthwhile when we succeed in freeing
one another to exercise our gifts without thought of status
or seniority. Then the Body is built up, and sees at the
centre of its life a model for ministry.

4. *We must reciprocate ministry to one another.*
Traditionally this is not the way we operate. Ministry is
usually expected to flow one way, from the pastor to the
people. But who looks after the pastors? Who listens to
their aches? How do they keep fresh? Again, the
traditional answers have been for the clergymen to keep a
stiff upper lip and pretend he has no problems. Or to look
to a friend or confessor outside the parish. Or to rely on an
occasional retreat. But how much better to have a fellowship of leadership within the parish, where joys and
sorrows can be shared, and rebukes given and accepted in
love.

Our own pastoral leadership has many shortcomings,
but it has proved its worth abundantly in reciprocal
ministry. We have had some hilarious times together. I
believe that we have all, on occasion, broken down and
wept. Certainly I have been more ministered to than I have
ministered in such a group. I have been wonderfully sustained and painfully rebuked. Members have loved me
enough to tell me my faults, and to help me come to terms
with them. Rebuke like this is costly to give, and costly to
receive. But it makes for growth. I would hate to go back to
the old way of apparent invulnerability and pretended competence. I know I am a weak and sinful man: I need my
close partners in leadership to help me grow and to offset
my inadequacies and stupidities.

Such community of leadership is rare, but it need not
be. It can happen anywhere. All that is needed is for the
ordained minister to gather round him a small group of
committed Christians who will love and disciple one
another. He pours himself into such a group. They share
much of their lives together. Financial, ministerial, personal, matrimonial issues can be worked over together. All

are enriched. And the pattern of servant leadership begins to emerge.

Enabling leadership

It is one thing to recognise that the function of Christian leadership is to equip members of the congregation for their ministry. It is quite another actually to do it. How can we enable people to discover their gifts, and use them for the common good?

1. *We can equip by teaching.* It is deeply entrenched in the mind of the average Christian that ministry is the role of the paid professional. Therefore constant teaching on the importance and usefulness of every limb in the Body is essential. The leadership needs repeatedly to expose the congregation to the biblical truth that all, and not some, Christians are ministers of Christ. It is unfortunately so revolutionary a concept that it will take time to get assimilated.

2. *We can equip by modelling.* It is no good the vicar preaching every member ministry if he persists in doing everything of significance in the church himself. To be sure, many parishioners will not feel they have been visited if the vicar does not come in person. But he will be doing them a long term service by training a team of lay visitors who can effectively cover a small area regularly and build up relationships with those in their street, particularly if the visiting is seen as the responsibility of the Fellowship Group in the area. Members of the congregation may well be shocked to find the vicar sitting in the pew with his wife occasionally, and a lay leader taking the Sunday service. But they will see that he means business about every member ministry. We must not only teach, but demonstrate that the church does not consist of one member but many; that all are called to serve; and that a number are called to lead.

3. *We can equip by discipling.* Jesus did this with the twelve, and more intensively with Peter, James and John.

Barnabas did it with Saul of Tarsus. He and Saul did it with John Mark – and so did Simon Peter. John had a school of disciples around him in Ephesus. The craftsmen of the Middle Ages each had their group of apprentices. And yet this method of encouraging gifts and ministries is strangely neglected in the modern church. Paul charged Timothy, his own erstwhile apprentice, 'what you have heard from me among many witnesses entrust to faithful men who will be able to teach others also' (2 Timothy 2:2). It is highly effective in producing the next generation of leaders, as many of the para-church organisations like Navigators and even sects like Mormons have been quick to recognise.

4. *We can equip by exposure.* People frequently have no idea of their gifts until they are exposed to some situation, and encouraged to launch out. I think of a gifted young evangelist who had no idea he possessed such a gift until he brought someone to me and asked me to show him the way to a living faith. I said, 'No: you are his friend. You show him.' He did, and he has been doing it ever since. I think of someone with a gentle singing voice. 'I could never sing a solo in church,' she felt. But one day she launched out in faith. God used her: and she now has a real ministry in song. I think of a group of young people who launched out into leading the prayers one night in church. It showed them they could lead people much older than themselves. I think of a man with a budding prophetic gift. Once the plunge was taken and he had spoken, however hesitantly, in church, he developed rapidly. And I think of my own life. I know that I have grown most when I have been thrust into situations where I had to attempt some sort of ministry though aware I was totally ill-equipped for it. We get equipped by exposure.

In his remarkable book *Dedication and Leadership*, Douglas Hyde, communist turned Christian, has this to say:

> The instruction of a new Party member does not normally begin immediately after he joins. Quite deliberately, and with good reason, the Party sends its new

members, wherever possible, into some form of public activity *before instruction begins.*[1]

This is precisely the principle adopted by Jesus. He told Peter to follow him in order to become a fisher of men. His 'come and see' invitation was followed by 'go and tell'. Jesus sent out his disciples to tell others long before they were ready, by our standards. They learned fast, as they engaged in practical service.

How unlike the modern church, where large numbers gather and listen to one person exercising his preaching gift, while the vast majority passively listen (or slumber). Seldom is anyone trusted with any ministry until he has been a Christian for some years and proved himself. Little is expected of the new Christian until he has sat and listened and grown enough to mature. What fools we are! It is hard to imagine how a church structure could be better designed to frustrate initiative and discourage the gifts of members than the structures common to our mainline denominations. By contrast, the new believers at Thessalonica were left to fend for themselves and provide their own incipient leadership a mere three weeks after being evangelised by Paul. That is exactly how the gospel has spread so fast among the Quichua Indians of Colombia in recent years: the converts were entrusted with leadership. Indeed, all over the Third World, church growth, under young and supposedly ill trained leaders, has long surpassed that in Europe and the United States!

5. *We can equip by means of house groups.* The group in the home is a superb place to discover and encourage the gifts and ministries of church members. In the intimacy of the home group people will venture into an area of ministry which they would never attempt in public. It may be letter writing to a missionary, or playing a guitar in worship, or making the supper for the group. It is important to encourage everyone to undertake some activity in the group. Indeed, encouragement in general is of the utmost importance. 'We know in part and we prophesy in part' wrote Paul (1 Cor. 13). He might well have added that *all* our gifts

and ministries are partial and imperfect. People need to be encouraged to experiment, and to accept instruction and, if necessary, correction. 'Trust God, and have a try' is much better advice than 'Attempt nothing unless you are sure you can do it.' It is not only prophecy, but every other gift that needs to be exercised 'according to the measure of faith' (Rom. 12:3). This lays on Christian leaders the responsibility of creating a climate of expectation that God will use the most unlikely people, and of willingness for mistakes to be made and accepted in love. When people feel secure, then they are prepared to experiment. It is in this way that they generally discover what are and what are not their gifts.

At least once a year it is good to have an evening when members share what they would really love to do in Christ's service. Our own spiritual desires are often an indication of potential gifts. Another evening should be given to affirming one another. 'What I most appreciate about you is . . . ' Often people are astonished to discover gifts in this way. And gifts discovered and tested in the small group may subsequently become important to the church at large. Whether they do or not, the member concerned has found a ministry, and the leadership has fulfilled its role by helping to bring this about.

6. *We can equip by involvement*. Everyone who is doing anything in the church should be equipped to do it better. And everyone who has received training should be given a sphere in which to exercise it. These are two aspects of training by involvement which are crucial to hold together.

We in Oxford are very much at the learning stage in all this. We do not yet equip all active members of our church to exercise their gifts better. And we often fail to involve them practically after training has been undergone. However we lay considerable store by an annual training course. It takes an evening a month for three months. It includes two full day conferences on a Saturday, and is followed by a weekend of ministry in some nearby parish.

The course is by invitation only, and can be run either

by the parish staff or, better, on a local ecumenical basis.
Each evening consists of a time of worship, led by the
participants; a time of sustained teaching; coffee or a meal;
and the last part of the evening in tutor groups, where the
topic may be tackled by guided discussion, role-play, or
some other method. Each member of the group spends two
personal sessions with the tutor, and is put through his
paces by means of a 'dry run' of counselling, of personal
evangelism, and of handling some great subject like suffering, with an imaginary enquirer. Each member of the
group will speak under supervision at some church gathering, however small. And during the weekend away, some
will lead a service, some pray or give testimony in public,
some lead a house group, some address teenagers. Often
an evangelistic addresss brings the mini-mission to an end,
and that gives the chance for members of the course to
counsel enquirers and help them through to assurance in
Christ. Needless to say, many gifts emerge and much
growth takes place on a course like this. It is our annual
basic training course, and we prize it highly. It leads on to
various other small courses: on controversial doctrinal
issues, on public speaking, on counselling and on the
leadership of small groups, especially Fellowship Groups.

Many congregations will feel that they are unable to
mount anything of the sort. Many clergy will feel that they
do not have that type of talent in their church. I have a
suspicion that both are wrong. The Lord gives gifts to his
church, and those gifts include the various ministries we
have been talking of (Eph. 4:11, 12). If we doubt this, we
doubt the Lord.

Management or ministry?

In the vast majority of churches models of ministry are
frankly managerial, if they exist at all. The ordained man is
the acknowledged leader of the enterprise. If he is lucky he
has an assistant. But he is in the driving seat. That is what
he has been trained to attempt. That is what the congregations have been trained to expect. Can such ingrained
attitudes change? Is the model of servant leadership,

demonstrated and required by Jesus, too threatening, too demanding?

Change is certainly possible, if all concerned are prepared to pay the price. It is really a matter of attitude. If the clergyman even in a small country parish is gripped by the New Testament vision of every limb in the Body working properly and making its own special contribution, then he can enable it to happen. It lies very much in his hands. To be sure, he may have to counteract the weight of tradition. He may have to go against 'what has always been done'. But if he believes that all are called to serve, if he believes that presbyters should be a team and not an individual, if he believes that the potential for Christian ministry lies slumbering there in the pews waiting to be mobilised, he can act: indeed he must. And he does not need to wait for changes in the laws of the Church.

I know of no Church law to prevent the rector gathering round him a group of people with whom he shares the oversight of the congregation. I know of no Church law to prevent training courses figuring strongly in the programme of a church, so that the saints are built up for service. I know of no Church law to prevent men and women within the congregation from sharing in leading the worship, the evangelism, the teaching, the counselling, the house groups and from assisting in administering the Holy Communion. Why should the vicar chair the Parochial Church Council or indeed his own staff meeting? I do not chair either of them. There are others better able to do it. Let them exercise their ministry for the good of the bodies concerned. Why should the rector administer the parish if there are others with greater organisational skills to do so? Why should we not form a mixed leadership team of men and women, ordained and lay within our parishes? I know of no reason except for inertia, inherited prejudice and fear.

Perhaps fear is the strongest of these; fear that it might be too radical, fear that the incumbent would not have anything left to do, fear of the invasion of cherished areas of monopoly. In point of fact these fears are groundless. Perfect love casts out fear, and when that love runs throughout the Body such fears are wont to disappear. It may be radical to encourage the gifts of all within the priestly Body of Christ; but it is biblical, and it works. It only seems radical because we have been disobedient so long. And as for the fear that the trained man, the parson, will be unemployed if others are equipped to minister, this does not happen. They will cover far more ground between them than he as a single person ever could. He will therefore be faced with more problems and be called upon for more guidance in more lively and challenging situations than he has ever known before in his life. Moreover, since he has donned the apron of the Servant he will find that others in the leadership don it too. No longer will he be the isolated one-man minister. He will find himself in the centre of a loving team of servants. Others will serve him, just as he serves others. And the pattern of the supreme Servant of all will increasingly be seen in that congregation.

Is it too much to hope that some such manifestation of Servant ministry be widely seen in our Church in this country, before persistence in the present models of expensive male professionalism in diminishing congregations brings our beloved Church to bankruptcy and perhaps to dissolution? More than once in previous generations God has had to break what would not bend. Pray God it may not be so with us! He need not, if we apply the scriptural model of the Servant to this the most controversial and resistant of all areas within the church, her ordained ministry.

REFERENCES

Chapter 2

1. O. Cullmann, *The Christology of the New Testament,* S.C.M., p. 161.
2. J. Jeremias, *The Servant of God,* S.C.M., p. 98f.
3. T.W. Manson, *The Church's Ministry,* Hodder, p. 27.

Chapter 3

1. E. Brunner, *The Misunderstanding of the Church,* Lutterworth, p. 50.
2. M. Harper, *Let My People Grow,* Hodder.
3. J.B. Lightfoot, *The Christian Ministry,* Thynne and Jarvis, p. 5.
4. *Ibid,* p. 5.

Chapter 4

1. B. L. Manning, *A Layman in the Ministry,* Independent Press, p. 152.
2. D. Daube, *The New Testament and Rabbinic Judaism,* London, p. 244ff.
3. J. Jeremias, *Zeitschrift für die neutestamentlich Wissenschaft,* 1957, p. 130f.
4. Hugh Silvester, *The Theology of Ordination,* an unpublished paper.
5. Hans Küng, *Why Priests?,* Fontana, p. 67.
6. M. Harper, *op. cit.* p. 230.
7. E. Brunner, *op. cit.* chs. 7–10.

8. E. Schweizer, *Church Order in the New Testament*, S.C.M., p. 186.

Chapter 5

1. Cranmer, *Remains and Letters*, p. 305.
2. Hooper, *Later Writings*, p. 90.
3. Lightfoot, *op. cit.* p. 22.

Chapter 6

1. W. Telfer, *The Office of a Bishop*, D.L.T., p. 41.
2. A. T. Hanson, *The Pioneer Ministry*, S.C.M., p. 144.
3. *Christianity Divided*, ed. D. J. Callahan, Sheed and Ward, p.10.
4. See Cullmann's chapter 'The Tradition' in his *The Early Church*, S.C.M.
5. A. Ehrhardt, *The Apostolic Succession*, Lutterworth, p. 20.
6. See his article 'Apostle' in the Kittel *Wörterbuch zum Neuen Testament*.
7. This is acknowledged by Dix in *The Apostolic Ministry*, ed. K. E. Kirk, Hodder, p. 200.
8. Kirk in *The Apostolic Ministry*, p. 40
9. See E. Molland in the *Journal of Ecclesiastical History*, 1950, i, p. 12ff.
10. See W. Telfer in the *Journal of Ecclesiastical History*, 1952, iii, p. 1f.
11. T. M. Lindsay, *The Church and the Ministry in the Early Centuries*, Hodder, p. 279.
12. W. Telfer, *The Office of a Bishop*, D.L.T., p. 119.
13. Richard Hooker, *Ecclesiastical Polity*, 7.5.8, and 7.14.11.
14. This is extensively documented in Norman Sykes, *Old Priest and New Presbyter*, C.U.P.
15. Cited by N. Sykes, *op. cit.* p. 212.

Chapter 7

1. A. G. Hebert, *Ways of Worship*, cited in Lambeth Report (1958) 2.85.
2. Alan Richardson *Introduction to the Theology of the New Testament*, S.C.M., p. 201.
3. *Ibid*, p. 303.
4. Lightfoot, *op. cit.*, p. 123ff., Lindsay, *op. cit.* p. 308, Tertullian, *De Baptismo*, 5.
5. Chrysostom, *Homily on Hebrews*, 13.8.
6. This doctrine evoked John Knox's protest: 'Is there any oblivion or forgetfulness fallen on God the Father? Hath he forgotten the death and passion of Jesus Christ, so that he needs to be brought in memory thereof by any mortal man?'
7. B. F. Westcott, *The Epistle of the Hebrews*, Macmillan, p. 230.
8. Justin, *Dialogue*, 41.
9. Lightfoot, *op. cit.* p. 134.
10. Cranmer, *The Lord's Supper*, Thynne, v. 11.
11. *Ibid*. v. 3.
12. Hooker, *op. cit.* v. 78.

Chapter 8

1. See Clement of Alexandria, *Stromateis*, 3.18.
2. *Women and Holy Orders*, p. 126.

Chapter 9

1. See Ronald Higgins, *The Seventh Enemy*, Hodder.

Chapter 10

1. Douglas Hyde, *Dedication and Leadership*, Notre Dame, p. 42.

Michael Green

WHY BOTHER WITH JESUS?

'Why bother?' considers Michael Green, is a widespread disease. Nothing seems to matter any more so long as we have our rise in wages, so long as the cost of our comforts is not too high, so long as we have a colour telly.

The disease has taken hold of our concern for the truth. When matters of right and wrong are settled by head-count rather than principle, a moral collapse could well be in the offing.

From this grim diagnosis Michael Green asks 'Why Bother with Jesus?', looking in detail at the qualities in Jesus which make us want to learn more about him.

Michael Green

YOU MUST BE JOKING

Will you stand out from the crowd, and think for yourself?
Will you have the courage to examine the evidence and ask
yourself how sound are the assumptions about God and
meaning, life and death, with which you have lived so far?

'I have collected here,' writes Michael Green, 'a number of
very common assumptions about the most important issues
in life. These assumptions sound good, but they won't do.
They are dangerous fallacies, and offer no proper
foundation for life. Time and again when folk have brought
them forward I have felt (or said), "You must be joking!" '

Michael Green

TO CORINTH WITH LOVE

The fires of controversy still burn bright, just as they did in the early church. Whatever the context, the Apostle Paul tackled the thorniest issues squarely, and with authority. It is his letters to the Corinthian Church, Michael Green believes and demonstrates, which provide crucial insights into a whole cluster of today's most difficult issues.

John Perry

CHRISTIAN LEADERSHIP

Good leaders, John Perry believes, are largely made, not born. But many Christians are too hesitant and inert, not believing that they have anything to give. The causes of such reticence must be faced if the local church is to prosper. In particular, the dearth of men in many churches must not be neglected: new strategies are needed to use their gifts and meet their needs.

Realistic about the difficulties, frustrations and temptations, encouraging about the opportunities, *Christian Leadership* makes an insistent plea for a higher quality of spiritual leadership which will strengthen the church and increase its impact on society.

John Perry is Warden of the Lee Abbey Community.

Charles Swindoll

IMPROVING YOUR SERVE

Christ's call to unselfish living

How can anyone be a genuine servant in today's 'look out for number one' world? What sort of dangers, rewards and internal struggles are involved?

As Charles Swindoll studied Christian servanthood, he was amazed at the new depths and insights God revealed. 'With remarkable regularity the Lord turned on the lights in areas that had been obscure or dark in my thinking throughout my Christian life. Becoming a servant began to be something beautiful, yes, essential, rather than something fearful and weird. I not only desired it for myself (a process that is still going on), but I wanted to share with others what God was revealing to me?